The Westminster Confession of Faith

The Westminster Confession of Faith

An Authentic Modern Version

Summertown Texts
Signal Mountain, Tennessee

Revised Second Edition
1984
ISBN: 0-9614303-0-3

Styled, designed, and otherwise prepared to the point of printing by Ampersand, Ltd. (Art Director: Janet Katz). Cover by Philip Rollinson.

Printed in the United States of America by Bagpipe Press, Inc.

Contents

Introduction

Few people in the English-speaking world today would question the value of modern translations of Holy Scripture into currently spoken English. Although the Authorized (King James) Version of 1611 will always retain its place as a classic translation of beauty and nobility, it is being superseded in daily use by more modern translations. There have been so many changes in the English language in the past 350 years that many people find seventeenth-century English prose difficult to understand. The Westminster Confession of Faith was formulated in the 1640's, only a generation after the King James Bible. It has become equally difficult to comprehend, an acute problem for the many officers in reformed churches who have taken vows binding them to the doctrines articulated in the Confession of Faith.

With the hope of remedying this situation we are offering here a modern version of the Westminster Confession, which attempts to be absolutely true to the full content of the original theology and at the same time to be clear and comprehensible to the ordinary church member of this generation. Our version of the Westminster text is, of course, merely a private translation and makes no claim to be the authorized work of any church. We simply offer it and the ancillary matter on the changes in the text and proof texts as tools for studying and understanding what many believe to be the greatest single statement of reformed Christian doctrine. We hope that laymen, churchmen, and scholars will find use for this work. Laymen not only need to know what the Westminister Confession actually says, but they also need to be aware of the changes which have taken place in the text and in the proof texts. Churchmen and scholars will also find this version of interest insofar as any translation is inevitably interpretive and hence a kind of commentary.

The changes which have been made to the original 1647 edition and which are reflected in the current American editions are significant but not too extensive. Both the Presbyterian Church in the United States of America (PCUSA, UPCUSA after the merger in 1958 with the United Presbyterian Church of North America) and the Presbyterian Church in the United States (PCUS), the two largest American Presbyterian denominations (now, of course, reunited since June 1983), added to the original 33, two new chapters, "Of the Holy Spirit" and "Of the Gospel of the Love of God and Missions" (PCUSA — simply entitled "Of the Gospel" in the identical PCUS version) in the twentieth century. PCUSA also added a "Declaratory Statement" interpreting the original Chapters 3 and 10, and both churches independently developed new versions of the original Chapter 24 on marriage. Our modern version is of the basic pre-1900 American text, which with a few exceptions is the same as the original British version of 1647. We have also included the two new Chapters 34 and 35 (9 and 10 in PCUS), the "Declaratory Statement," and the two new versions of Chapter 24 for comparison. We are indebted to the United Presbyterian Church in the United States of America and to the Presbyterian Church in the United States for permission to reproduce their twentieth-century additions and changes.

In addition to these comparative textual inclusions, Appendix I discusses and systematically lists all the changes from the original text of 1647. Appendix II does the same thing for the proof texts, which have also undergone independent major revision by both PCUSA and PCUS. Using Appendix II, the reader will readily be able to identify all the proof texts which are now or have been used to support a particular statement or section and to recognize the status of each citation, whether added, retained, or deleted, and by which Church body.

We hope then that this work will have widespread use among professional churchmen and laymen, among scholars and ordinary readers. As for the defects and errors, which we suspect exist in spite of our efforts and desire that they did not, we can only ask for charitable forgiveness. We want to express our particular gratitude to Mayme Tyler for typing and other clerical assistance and to Ann Rollinson for clerical help and patient encouragement.

The Westminster Confession of Faith

Chapter 1

Concerning Holy Scripture

1. Our natural understanding and the works of creation and providence so clearly show God's goodness, wisdom, and power that human beings have no excuse for not believing in Him.[1] However, these means alone cannot provide that knowledge of God and of His will which is necessary for salvation.[2] Therefore it pleased the Lord at different times and in various ways to reveal Himself and to declare that this revelation contains His will for His church.[3] Afterwards it pleased God to put this entire revelation into writing so that the truth might be better preserved and transmitted and that the church, confronted with the corruption of the flesh and the evil purposes of Satan and the world, might be more securely established and comforted.[4] Since God no longer reveals Himself to His people in those earlier ways,[6] Holy Scripture is absolutely essential.[5]

2. What we call Holy Scripture or the written word of God now includes all the books of the Old and the New Testament, which are:

The Old Testament

Genesis	II Chronicles	Daniel
Exodus	Ezra	Hosea
Leviticus	Nehemiah	Joel
Numbers	Esther	Amos
Deuteronomy	Job	Obadiah
Joshua	Psalms	Jonah
Judges	Proverbs	Micah
Ruth	Ecclesiastes	Nahum
I Samuel	Song of Solomon	Habakkuk
II Samuel	Isaiah	Zephaniah
I Kings	Jeremiah	Haggai
II Kings	Lamentations	Zechariah
I Chronicles	Ezekial	Malachi

3

The New Testament

Matthew	Ephesians	Hebrews
Mark	Philippians	James
Luke	Colossians	I Peter
John	I Thessalonians	II Peter
Acts	II Thessalonians	I John
Romans	I Timothy	II John
I Corinthians	II Timothy	III John
II Corinthians	Titus	Jude
Galatians	Philemon	Revelation

All of these books are inspired by God and are the rule of faith and life.[6a]

3. The books usually called the Apocrypha are not divinely inspired and are not part of the canon of Scripture. They therefore have no authority in the church of God and are not to be valued or used as anything other than human writings.[7]

4. The Bible speaks authoritatively and so deserves to be believed and obeyed. This authority does not depend on the testimony of any man or church but completely on God, its author, Who is Himself truth. The Bible therefore is to be accepted as true, because it is the word of God.[8]

5. We may be influenced by the testimony of the church to value the Bible highly and reverently, and Scripture itself shows in so many ways that it is God's word; for example, in its spiritual subject matter, in the effectiveness of its teaching, the majesty of its style, the agreement of all its parts, its unified aim from beginning to end (to give all glory to God), the full revelation it makes of the only way of man's salvation, its many other incomparably outstanding features, and its complete perfection. However, we are completely persuaded and assured of the infallible truth and divine authority of the Bible only by the inward working of the Holy Spirit, Who testifies by and with the word in our hearts.[9]

6. The whole purpose of God about everything pertaining to His own glory and to man's salvation, faith, and life is either explicitly stated in the Bible or may be deduced as inevitably and logically following from it.[10] Nothing is at any time to be added to the Bible, either from new revelations of the Spirit or from traditions of men.[11] Nevertheless we do recognize that the inward illumination of the Spirit of God is necessary for a saving understanding of the things which are revealed in the word.[12] We also recognize that some provisions for the worship of God and the government of the church are similar to secular activities and organizations; these are to be directed according to our natural understanding and our Christian discretion and should conform to the general rules of the word, which are always to be observed.[13]

7. The meanings of all the passages in the Bible are not equally obvious, nor is any individual passage equally clear to everyone.[14] However, everything which we have to know, believe, and observe in order to be saved is so clearly presented and revealed somewhere in the Bible that the uneducated as well as the educated can sufficiently understand it by the proper use of the ordinary means of grace.[15]

8. The Old Testament in Hebrew (the native language of the ancient people of God) and the New Testament in Greek (the language most widely known internationally at the time the New Testament was written) were directly inspired by God[16] and have been kept uncontaminated throughout time by His special care and providence. They are therefore authentic and are to be the church's ultimate source of appeal in every religious controversy.[17] The original languages of the Bible, however, are not understood by all of God's people. But all of God's people have a right to the Bible, and God Himself commands them to read it thoroughly with awe and reverence for Him.[18] Consequently the Bible should be translated into the native language of every people to whom it is introduced. Then, the word of God will live fully in everyone; everyone will be able to worship God in an acceptable way; and all believers may have hope through the endurance and the encouragement of the Bible.[19]

9. The infallible standard for the interpretation of the Bible is the Bible itself. And so any question about the true and complete sense of a passage in the Bible (which is a unified whole) can be answered by referring to other passages which speak more plainly.[20]

10. The Holy Spirit speaking in the Bible is the supreme judge of all religious controversies, all decisions of religious councils, all the opinions of ancient writers, all human teachings, and every private opinion.[21] We are to be satisfied with the judgment of Him Who is and can be the only judge.

Chapter 2

Concerning God and the Holy Trinity

1. There is only one living and true God,[1] Who is infinite in being and perfection,[2] a completely pure spirit,[3] invisible,[4] without body, parts, or emotions,[5] unchangeable,[6] immensely vast,[7] eternal,[8] limitless,[9] almighty,[10] completely wise,[11] completely holy,[12] completely free,[13] and completely absolute.[14] He works everything according to the purpose of His own unchangeable and completely righteous will[15] for His own glory.[16] He is completely loving,[17] gracious, merciful, and long-suffering. He overflows with goodness and truth. He forgives wickedness, transgression, and sin,[18] and rewards those who diligently seek Him.[19] His judgments are completely just and awesome;[20] He hates all sin[21] and will not acquit the guilty.[22]

2. God has all life, glory, goodness, and blessedness in and of Himself.[23] He alone is all-sufficient in and unto Himself, nor does He need any of His creations or derive any glory from them. Rather, He manifests His own glory in, by, unto, and on them.[24] He is the only source of all being, by Whom, through Whom, and to Whom everything exists.[25] He has completely sovereign dominion over all things and does with, to, or for them whatever He pleases.[26] Everything is revealed and completely open to Him.[27] His knowledge is infinite, infallible, and does not depend on any created being,[28] so that to Him nothing is conditional or uncertain.[29] He is completely holy in all His purposes, works, and commands.[30] To Him is due whatever worship, service, or obedience He is pleased to require from angels, human beings, and all other creatures.[31]

3. In the unity of the Godhead there are three persons, having one substance, power, and eternity: God the Father, God the Son, and God the Holy Spirit.[32] The Father exists. He is not generated and does not come from any source. The Son is eternally generated from the Father,[33] and the Holy Spirit eternally comes from the Father and the Son.[34]

Chapter 3

Concerning God's Eternal Decrees

1. From all eternity and by the completely wise and holy purpose of His own will, God has freely and unchangeably ordained whatever happens.[1] This ordainment does not mean, however, that God is the author of sin (He is not),[2] that He represses the will of His created beings, or that He takes away the freedom or contingency of secondary causes. Rather, the will of created beings and the freedom and contingency of secondary causes are established by Him.[3]

2. Although God knows whatever may or can happen under all possible circumstances,[4] He has not ordered anything because He foresaw it in the future as something which would happen under such circumstances.[5]

3. In order to manifest His glory God has ordered that some men and angels should be predestined to everlasting life[6] and that others should be foreordained to everlasting death.[7]

4. This predestination and foreordination of angels and men is precise and unchangeable. The number and identity of angels and men in each group is certain, definite, and unalterable.[8]

5. Before the creation of the world,[9] according to His eternal, unchangeable plan[10] and the hidden purpose and good pleasure of His will,[11] God has chosen in Christ[12] those of mankind who are predestined to life and to everlasting glory.[13] He has done this solely out of His own mercy and love and completely to the praise of His wonderful grace.[15] This choice was completely independent of His foreknowledge of how His created beings would be or act. Neither their faith nor good works had any part in influencing His selection.[14]

6. Just as God has determined that the elect shall be glorified, so, too, in the eternal and completely free purpose of His will He has foreordained all the means by which that election is accomplished.[16] And so, those who are chosen, having fallen in Adam, are redeemed by Christ.[17] They are effectually called to faith in Christ by His Spirit working in them at the right time,[18] and they are justified,[19] adopted,[20] sanctified,[21] and kept by His power through faith unto salvation.[22] Only the elect,

7

and no others, are redeemed by Christ, effectually called, justified, adopted, sanctified, and saved.[23]

7. According to the hidden purpose of His own will, by which He offers or withholds mercy at His pleasure, and for the glory of His sovereign power over His creatures, it pleased God not to call the rest of mankind[24] and to ordain them to dishonor and wrath for their sin,[25] to the praise of His glorious justice.[26]

8. This important and mysterious doctrine of predestination must be treated with special discretion and care, so that, paying attention to and obeying the will of God revealed in His word, men may be assured that they have been eternally chosen from the certainty of their effectual calling. In this way the doctrine of predestination will elicit not only our praise, reverence, and admiration for God, but also a humble and diligent life, fully supporting everyone who sincerely obeys the gospel.[27]

Chapter 4

Concerning Creation

1. In the beginning it pleased God the Father, Son, and Holy Spirit,[1a] to create the world out of nothing in order to reveal the glory of His eternal power, wisdom, and goodness.[1b] He made everything in the world, visible and invisible, in the space of six days, and it was very good.[1]

2. After God had made all the other creatures, He created man, male and female,[2] with reasoning, immortal souls.[3] He endowed them with knowledge, righteousness, and true holiness in His own image[4] and wrote His law in their hearts.[5] God also gave them the ability to obey His law and the potential to disobey it; i.e., He gave them freedom of their own will, which could change.[6] In addition to this law written in their hearts, they were commanded not to eat from the Tree of the Knowledge of Good and Evil.[7] As long as they obeyed God's law and kept this commandment, they were happy in fellowship with God[8] and had dominion over the other creatures.[9]

Chapter 5

Concerning Providence

1. God, Who created everything, also upholds everything. He directs, regulates, and governs every creature, action, and thing, from the greatest to the least,[1] by His completely wise and holy providence.[2] He does so in accordance with His infallible foreknowledge[3] and the voluntary, unchangeable purpose of His own will,[4] all to the praise of the glory of His wisdom, power, justice, goodness, and mercy.[5]

2. God is the first cause, and in relationship to Him everything happens unchangeably and infallibly.[6] However, by this same providence, He orders things to happen from secondary causes. As a result of these secondary causes, some things must inevitably happen;[7] others may or may not happen depending on the voluntary intentions of the agents involved; and some things do not have to happen but may, depending on other conditions.[8]

3. God uses ordinary means to work out His providence day by day.[9] But, as He pleases,[12] He may work without,[10] beyond,[11] or contrary to these means.

4. God's providence reveals His almighty power, unknowable wisdom, and infinite goodness. His providence extends even to the fall[13] and to all other sins of angels and men.[14] These sins are not simply allowed by God, but are bound,[15] ordered, and governed by Him in the fulness of His wisdom and power so that they fulfill His own holy purposes.[16] However, the sinfulness still belongs to the creature and does not proceed from God, whose holy righteousness does not and cannot cause or approve sin.[17]

5. In the fulness of His wisdom, righteousness, and grace God often allows His own children to be tempted in various ways and for a time to pursue the corruption of their own hearts. God does this to chastise them for their previous sins and to reveal to them the hidden strength of corruption and deceitfulness in their hearts, so that they may be humbled.[18] In addition to various other just and holy results, believers are thereby raised to a closer and more constant dependence on God for their support and are also made more alert in detecting and resisting

opportunities to sin.[19]

6. It is different for the wicked and the ungodly. As punishment for their previous sins, God, the righteous judge, spiritually blinds and hardens them in their own sinfulness.[20] From them God not only withdraws His grace, by which they might have been spiritually enlightened,[21] but sometimes He also withdraws whatever gift of spiritual understanding they already had[22] and deliberately exposes them to the opportunities for sinning which their corrupt nature naturally seeks.[23] He thereby gives them over to their own desires, to the temptations of the world, and to the power of Satan,[24] and so it happens that they harden themselves even under those circumstances which God uses to soften others.[25]

7. Just as the providence of God in general extends to every creature, so, in a very special way it takes care of His church and orders all things for its good.[26]

Chapter 6

Concerning the Fall of Man, Sin, and the Punishment for Sin

1. Our first parents were led astray by the cunning temptation of Satan and sinned in eating the forbidden fruit.[1] It pleased God to allow them to sin, because in His wisdom and holiness He planned to order their sin to His own glory.[2]

2. By this sin they fell from their original righteousness and fellowship with God,[3] and so became dead in sin[4] and completely polluted in all their faculties and parts of body and soul.[5]

3. Since Adam and Eve are the root of all mankind, the guilt for this sin has been imputed to all human beings,[6] who are their natural descendants and have inherited the same death in sin and the same corrupt nature.[7]

4. This original corruption completely disinclines, incapacitates, and turns us away from every good, while it completely inclines us to every evil.[8] From it proceed all actualized sins.[9]

5. During life on earth this corrupt nature remains in those who are regenerated,[10] and, although it is pardoned and deadened in Christ, yet it and all its impulses are truly and properly sinful.[11]

6. Every sin, both original and actual, transgresses the righteous law of God and brings guilt on the sinner.[12] Every sinner is consequently subjected to the wrath of God,[13] the curse of the law,[14] and death,[15] with all the resultant miseries, spiritual, temporal, and eternal.[16]

Chapter 7

Concerning God's Covenant with Man

1. The distance between God and His creation is so great, that, although reasoning creatures owe Him obedience as their creator, they nonetheless could never realize any blessedness or reward from Him without His willingly condescending to them. And so it pleased God to provide for man by means of covenants.[1]

2. The first covenant made with man was a covenant of works.[2] In it life was promised to Adam and through him to his descendants,[2a] on the condition of perfect, personal obedience.[3]

3. By his fall, man made himself incapable of life under that covenant, and so the Lord made a second, the covenant of grace.[4] In it He freely offers sinners life and salvation through Jesus Christ. In order to be saved He requires faith in Jesus[5] and promises to give His Holy Spirit to everyone who is ordained to life so that they may be willing and able to believe.[6]

4. This covenant of grace is frequently identified in Scripture as a testament, in reference to the death of Jesus Christ, the testator, and to the everlasting inheritance and everything included in that legacy.[6a]

5. This covenant was administered differently in the time of the law and in the time of the gospel.[7] Under the law it was administered by promises, prophecies, sacrifices, circumcision, the paschal lamb, and other types and ordinances given to the Jewish people, all foreshadowing Christ.[8] For that time the covenant administered under the law through the operation of the Spirit was sufficient and effective in instructing the elect and building up their faith in the promised Messiah,[9] by Whom they had full remission of their sins and eternal salvation. This administration is called the Old Testament.[10]

6. Under the gospel Christ Himself, the substance [10a] of God's grace, was revealed. The ordinances of this New Testament are the preaching of the word and the administration of the sacraments of baptism and the Lord's supper.[11] Although these are fewer in number and are administered with more simplicity and less outward glory, yet they are available to all nations, Jews and Gentiles,[13] and in them the spiritual

power of the covenant of grace is more fully developed.[12] There are not then two essentially different covenants of grace, but one and the same covenant under different dispensations.[14]

Chapter 8

Concerning Christ the Mediator

1. In His eternal purpose it pleased God to choose and ordain the Lord Jesus, His only begotten Son, to be the mediator between God and man.[1] Jesus is the prophet,[2] priest,[3] and king,[4] the head and savior of His church,[5] the heir of all things,[6] and judge of the world.[7] From all eternity God gave Him a people to be His seed[8] and to be in time redeemed, called, justified, sanctified, and glorified by Him.[9]

2. The Son of God, the second person of the Trinity, is truly the eternal God, of one substance and equal with the Father. In the fulness of time He took on Himself the nature of man,[10] with all the essential qualities and ordinary frailties of man — except that He was sinless.[11] Jesus was conceived by the power of the Holy Spirit in the womb of the Virgin Mary out of her substance.[12] These two complete, perfect, and distinct natures, the Godhead and the manhood, were inseparably joined together in the one person of Jesus without being altered, disunited or jumbled.[13] The person Jesus is truly God and truly man, yet one Christ, the only mediator between God and man.[14]

3. His human nature being thus united to the divine, the Lord Jesus was sanctified and anointed with the Holy Spirit beyond all measure.[15] He had in Him all the treasures of wisdom and knowledge,[16] and in Him it pleased the Father that all fulness should dwell.[17] God's purpose was that Jesus, being holy, harmless, undefiled, and full of grace and truth, should be completely equipped to execute the office of mediator and guarantor.[18] Jesus did not take this office on Himself but was called to it by His Father,[19] Who gave and commanded Him to use all power and judgment.[20]

4. The Lord Jesus undertook this office completely voluntarily.[21] In order to discharge it He was made under[22] and perfectly fulfilled the law.[23] He endured extremely severe torment in His soul[24] and extremely painful suffering in His body.[25] He was crucified and died.[26] He was buried and remained under the power of death, but His body did not decay.[27] On the third day He arose from the dead[28] with the same body in which He suffered[29] and with which He also ascended into heaven.

There He sits at the right hand of His Father,[30] interceding for believers.[31] He will return to judge men and angels at the end of the world.[32]

5. By His perfect obedience and sacrifice, offered up to God once and for all through the eternal Spirit, the Lord Jesus has completely satisfied the justice of His Father[33] and purchased not only reconciliation but also an everlasting inheritance in the kingdom of heaven for everyone whom the Father has given to Him.[34]

6. Although the work of redemption was not actually done by Christ until after His incarnation, yet the power, effectiveness, and benefits of it were given to the elect in all ages from the beginning of the world by means of those promises, types, and sacrifices which revealed Him and indicated that He would be the seed of the woman, would bruise the serpent's head, and was the lamb slain from the beginning of the world. Jesus Christ is yesterday and today and forever the same.[35]

7. In the work of mediation Christ acts according to both His natures, each nature doing what is proper to each.[36] However, because of the unity of His person Scripture sometimes attributes what is proper to one nature to the person indicated by the other nature.[37]

8. Christ insures with absolute certainty that everyone for whom He purchased redemption actually accepts and receives it.[38] He makes intercession for them,[39] reveals the mysteries of salvation to them in and by the word,[40] and effectively persuades them to believe and obey by His Spirit. He governs their hearts by His word and Spirit[41] and overcomes all their enemies by His almighty power and wisdom in such ways as are most in agreement with His wonderful and unknowable administration of things.[42]

Chapter 9

Concerning Free Will

1. God has given man a will, which by nature is free, i.e., it is not forced or necessarily inclined toward good or evil.[1]

2. In his state of innocence man had complete freedom and the natural ability to will and to do what is good and pleasing to God.[2] God also made man so that he could lose that freedom.[3]

3. Man fell into a state of sin by his disobedience and so completely lost his ability to will any spiritual good involving salvation.[4] Consequently fallen man is by nature completely opposed to spiritual good,[5] is dead in sin,[6] and is unable by his own strength either to convert himself or to prepare himself for conversion.[7]

4. When God converts a sinner and brings him into a state of grace, He frees him from his natural enslavement to sin. By God's grace alone, freely given, sinful man is enabled to will and to do what is spiritually good.[8] However, since the old sinful nature also remains, the believer cannot consistently or perfectly will to do what is good but also wills evil.[9]

5. The will of man is perfectly free and permanently inclined to good alone only in the state of glory.[10/11]

Chapter 10

Concerning Effectual Calling

1. At the right time, appointed by Him, God effectually calls all those and only those whom He has predestined to life. He calls them by His word and Spirit out of their natural state of sin and death into grace and salvation through Jesus Christ.[1] He enlightens their minds spiritually with a saving understanding of the things of God.[2] He takes away their heart of stone and gives them a heart of flesh.[3] He renews their wills and by His almighty power leads them to what is good.[4] And so He effectually draws them to Jesus Christ.[5] But they come to Jesus voluntarily, having been made willing by God's grace.[6]

2. This effectual call is freely made by God and is entirely an act of His special grace. It does not depend on anything God foreknew or foresaw about the person called,[7] who is completely passive. God Himself gives life and renewal by the Holy Spirit.[8] He thereby enables each person to answer His call and to accept the grace He offers and actually gives.[9]

3. Elect infants, dying in infancy, are regenerated and saved by Christ through the Spirit,[9a] Who works when, where, and how He pleases.[9b] The same is true of all other elect persons who are incapable of being outwardly called by the ministry of the word.[10]

4. Others, not elect, may be called by the ministry of the word, and the Spirit may work in them in some of the same ways He works in the elect. However, they never truly come to Christ and therefore cannot be saved.[11] And, of course, people, not professing the Christian religion, cannot be saved in any other way at all,[12] no matter how hard they try to live a moral life according to their own understanding or try to follow the rules of some other religion. To say they can be saved is extremely harmful and should be denounced.[13]

Chapter 11

Concerning Justification

1. Those whom God effectually calls He also freely justifies.[14] He does not pour righteousness into them but pardons their sins and looks on them and accepts them as if they were righteous — not because of anything worked in them or done by them, but for Christ's sake alone. He does not consider their faith itself, the act of believing, as their righteousness or any other obedient response to the gospel on their part. Rather He imputes to them the obedience and judicial satisfaction earned by Christ.[15] For their part, they receive and rest on Christ and His righteousness by faith (and this faith is not their own but is itself a gift of God).[16]

2. Faith, thus receiving and resting on Christ and His righteousness, is the only means of justification.[17] In the person justified, however, it is always accompanied by all the other saving graces and is not a dead faith, but works by love.[18]

3. By His obedience and death Christ completely discharged the debt of all those who are so justified, and He made the correct, real, and full satisfaction to His Father's justice on their behalf.[19] Since Christ was voluntarily given by the Father for them,[20] and since His obedience and satisfaction were accepted in their place[21] and not for anything in them, their justification is the result only of His free grace[22] — so that both the perfect justice and the rich grace of God might be glorified in the justification of sinners.[23]

4. From all eternity God decreed the justification of all the elect,[24] and in the fulness of time Christ died for their sins and rose again for their justification.[25] Nevertheless, the elect are not justified until the Holy Spirit in due time does actually apply Christ to them.[26]

5. God continues to forgive the sins of those who are justified.[27] Although they can never fall from the state of justification,[28] they may by their sins come under God's fatherly displeasure and not have a sense of His presence with them until they humble themselves, confess their sins, ask for forgiveness, and renew their faith in repentance.[29]

6. The justification of believers under the Old Testament was in all these respects identical with the justification of believers under the New Testament.[30]

Chapter 12

Concerning Adoption

1. God guarantees the adoption of all those who are justified in and for the sake of His only son, Jesus Christ.[1] Those adopted enjoy the liberties and privileges of God's children,[2] have His name put on them,[3] receive the Spirit of adoption,[4] have access to the throne of grace with boldness,[5] and are enabled to cry, Abba, Father.[6] They are pitied,[7] protected,[8] provided for,[9] and disciplined by Him as a father.[10] They are never cast off, however,[11] and are sealed until the day of redemption[12] and inherit the promises[13] as heirs of everlasting salvation.[14]

Chapter 13

Concerning Sanctification

1. Those who are effectually called and regenerated have a new heart and a new spirit created in them. They are additionally sanctified, actually and personally, by the power of Christ's death and resurrection and by His word and Spirit dwelling in them.[1] The power of sin ruling over the whole body is destroyed,[2] and the desires of the old self are more and more weakened and killed.[3] At the same time the ability to practice true holiness, without which no one will see the Lord,[5] is brought to life and strengthened by all the saving graces.[4]

2. This sanctification works in the whole person,[6] but not completely or perfectly in this life. The old sinful nature retains some of its control in body, mind, and spirit. And so a continual and irreconcilable war goes on in every believer. The old nature tries to get its way in opposition to the Spirit, and the Spirit fights to assert its authority over the flesh.[7]

3. Although the old nature temporarily wins battles in this warfare,[8] the continual strengthening of the sanctifying Spirit of Christ enables the regenerate nature in each believer to overcome.[9] And so the saints grow in grace,[10] perfecting holiness in the fear of God.[11]

Chapter 14

Concerning Saving Faith

1. The gift of faith makes it possible for the souls of the elect to be saved by believing in Jesus Christ. This gift is the work of the Spirit of Christ in the hearts of the elect[1] and is ordinarily accomplished by the ministry of the word.[2] It is also increased and strengthened by the word, by prayer, and by the administration of the sacraments.[3]

2. By this faith a Christian believes whatever is revealed in the word to be the true, authentic, authoritative statement of God Himself.[4] By this faith the believer also acts according to what particular passages in the word say. By faith the believer humbly submits to and obeys God's various commands.[4a] He trembles at God's awesome threats,[4b] and eagerly embraces His promises about this life and the life to come.[4c] But the chief actions of saving faith are accepting, receiving, and resting on Christ alone for justification, sanctification, and eternal life, in the power of the covenant of grace.[4d]

3. This faith has different degrees of strength and weakness.[5] It may be attacked and weakened often and in many ways, but it gets the victory.[6] In many believers it matures and becomes completely assured through Christ,[7] Who both creates and perfects our faith.[8]

Chapter 15

Concerning Repentance Leading to Life

1. Repentance which leads to life is the blessed product of the gospel working in believers' lives.[1] Along with the doctrine of faith in Christ it is a doctrine to be preached by every minister of the gospel.[2]

2. In this repentance the sinner is able to see his sins as God sees them, as filthy and hateful, and as involving great danger to the sinner, because they are completely contrary to the holy nature and righteous law of God. Understanding that God in Christ is merciful to those who repent, the sinner suffers deep sorrow for and hates his sins, and so he determines to turn away from all of them. And turning to God,[3] he tries to walk with Him according to all His commandments.[4]

3. Although repentance is not any satisfaction for sin and does not cause the forgiveness of sins[5] (since forgiveness is an act of God's voluntary grace in Christ[6]), yet it is necessary to all sinners, and no one may expect to be forgiven without it.[7]

4. Just as there is no sin so small that it does not deserve damnation,[8] so there is no sin so great that it can bring damnation upon those who truly repent.[9]

5. Believers should not be satisfied with general repentance. Rather it is everyone's duty to try to repent of every individual sin individually.[10]

6. Everyone is also bound to confess privately his sins to God and to pray for forgiveness for them.[11] Confession, prayer for forgiveness, and the forsaking of sins which have been forgiven will find God's mercy.[12] Similarly, anyone who sins against his spiritual brother or the church should be willing to confess, privately or publicly, to demonstrate sorrow for his sin, and openly to state his repentance to those whom he has hurt.[13] They in turn are to be reconciled to him and to receive him in love.[14]

Chapter 16

Concerning Good Works

1. Good works are only those works identified as good by God and commanded by Him in His holy word.[1] They do not include other works, no matter how well-intentioned in design or zealously promoted by men.[2]

2. These good works, done in obedience to God's commandments, are the fruit and evidence of a true and living faith.[3] By them believers show their thankfulness,[4] strengthen their assurance of salvation,[5] edify their brothers in the Lord,[6] and become ornaments of all those who profess the gospel.[7] Good works in believers silence the criticism of the enemies of the gospel.[8] They also glorify God[9] by showing that believers are the workmanship and creation of Jesus Christ,[10] because their aim is that holiness of living which leads to eternal life.[11]

3. Believers get the ability to do good works entirely from the Spirit of Christ.[12] In addition to the other particular effects of God's grace already received, believers must be directed by the Holy Spirit in order to will and to do what pleases God.[13] However, they are not therefore to grow spiritually lazy, waiting for some special guidance from the Spirit before doing anything commanded by God. Rather, they should diligently attempt to identify what good works God has commanded in His word and then try their best to do all of them, praying earnestly and daily for the empowering and enabling of the Holy Spirit, Who lives in them.[14]

4. Those believers who do the best that can be done in obeying God in this life can never do more or even as much as He requires. Indeed they fall short of much which they are bound to do.[15]

5. We cannot, of course, by our best works deserve to be forgiven for our sins and to receive eternal life from God. There is that great disproportion between our best works in this life and the glory which is going to be revealed in us, and there is the infinite distance between us and God, Who does not profit from our best works and is not satisfied by them for the debt of our previous sins.[16] When we have done all we can,

we have only done our duty and are unprofitable servants.[17] Since the goodness of our best works in fact proceeds from His Spirit[18] and since, in so far as they are done by us, our best works are defiled and mixed with our weakness and imperfection, they cannot therefore even stand the scrutiny of God's judgment.[19]

6. Nevertheless, since the persons of believers are accepted through Christ, their good works in this life are also accepted in Him.[20] It is not as though they were perfect in God's sight[21] but that God, looking on them in His Son, is pleased to accept and reward what is sincerely done, even though accompanied by much weakness and imperfection.[22]

7. Works done by people who have not been spiritually reborn may be the same as those commanded by God and may be of good use to them and to others.[23] However, since they do not proceed from a heart purified by faith,[24] are not done in the right way, i.e., in response to God's word,[25] and are not done for the right purpose, the glory of God,[26] they are therefore sinful and cannot please God or make a person fit to receive grace from God.[27] Nevertheless, it is more sinful and displeasing to God not to do such works than to do them.[28]

Chapter 17

Concerning the Perseverance of the Saints

1. Those whom God has accepted in His Son and has effectually called and sanctified by His Spirit can never completely or finally fall out of their state of grace. Rather, they shall definitely continue in that state to the end and are eternally saved.[1]

2. This endurance of the saints does not depend on their own free will but on God's unchangeable decree of election, flowing from his voluntary, unchangeable love.[2] It also depends on the effectiveness of the merit and intercession of Jesus Christ,[3] on the indwelling Spirit and indwelling seed of God in the saints,[4] and on the nature of the covenant of grace.[5] All these establish the certainty and infallibility of their preservation.[6]

3. Nevertheless, the temptations of Satan, the world, and their old carnal nature, along with neglect of the means of their preservation, may lead believers to commit serious sins and to continue in them for a time.[7] They consequently displease God[8] and grieve His Holy Spirit,[9] have some of the fruit of God's grace and His comforts taken away from them,[10] have their hearts hardened[11] and their consciences wounded,[12] hurt and offend others,[13] and bring temporal judgments on themselves.[14]

Chapter 18

Concerning the Assurance of Grace and Salvation

1. Hypocrites and other unregenerate men may deceive themselves with false hopes and carnal presumptions about their being in God's favor and about their being saved.[1] Their presumptions will die with them.[2] However, those who truly believe in the Lord Jesus, who honestly love Him and try to walk in good conscience before Him, may in this life be assured with certainty that they are in a state of grace.[3] They may also rejoice in the hope of the glory of God, and they will never be ashamed of that hope.[4]

2. This certainty is not based on the fallible hope of guesswork or probabilities. Rather, it is the infallible assurance of faith,[5] established on the divine truth of the promises of salvation.[6] There is also the inner evidence of spiritual insight, given to us by God, to which these promises are directed.[7] And there is the testimony of the Spirit of adoption, witnessing with our spirits that we are the children of God.[8] This Spirit is the pledge of our inheritance. By Him we are sealed until the day of redemption.[9]

3. This infallible assurance is not so essential to faith that a true believer may not have doubts and conflicts about it, possibly wait some time for it, and grow into it.[10] But since the Spirit enables believers to know the things which are freely given to them by God, every believer may come to a full assurance of salvation by the ordinary working of the Spirit without unusual revelation.[11] Therefore it is every believer's duty to establish the certainty of his calling and election [11a] so that his heart may be filled with peace and joy in the Holy Spirit, with love and thankfulness to God, and with strength and cheerfulness of obedience. These are the true products of assurance,[11b] which is never conducive to an undisciplined life.[12]

4. The assurance true believers have of their salvation may be shaken, lessened, or interrupted for various reasons: from neglecting to preserve it; from committing some particular sin, which wounds the conscience and grieves the Spirit; from some sudden or strong temptation; or from God's withdrawing the sense of His presence and allowing them to walk

in darkness.[13] Nevertheless, they are never completely without God's seed, the life of faith, the love of Christ and of other believers, and the sincere heart and obedient conscience, out of which the Spirit may revive this assurance in due time[14] and by which they are in the meantime kept from complete despair.[15]

Chapter 19

Concerning the Law of God

1. God gave Adam a law as a covenant of works. He required Adam and all his descendants to obey this law, individually, completely, perpetually, and in precise accordance with its provisions. God promised life for keeping it and threatened death for disobeying it, and He gave man the power and ability to keep it. [1a]

2. After the fall this law continued to be a perfect rule of righteousness and was given, as such, by God on Mount Sinai in the ten commandments, written on two tablets.[1] The first four commandments establish our obligations to God and the remaining six our obligations to human beings.[2]

3. In addition to this law, ordinarily called the moral law, it pleased God to give the people of Israel, as a pre-Christian assembly of believers, ceremonial laws, containing many typical ordinances. Some of these ordinances pertain to worship and foreshadow Christ, His grace, actions, suffering, and the benefits to be had from believing in Him.[3] The rest of these ordinances contain various instructions about moral duties.[4] All of these ceremonial laws are now nullified under the New Testament.[5]

4. God also gave the Israelites, as a political body, various judicial laws. These expired with the state of Israel and make no further obligation on God's people than seems appropriate in contemporary legal codes.[6]

5. The moral law, however, does pertain to everyone, saved and unsaved, forever, not just with respect to its content but also in relationship to the authority of God, the Creator, Who gave it.[7] In the gospel Christ does not in any way remove this obligation, but rather strengthens it.[8]

6. Although true believers are not justified or condemned by the law as a covenant of works,[9] the law is nevertheless very useful to them and to others. As a rule of life, it informs them of God's will and of their obligation to obey it.[10] It also reveals to them the sinful pollution of their nature, hearts, and lives,[11] so that, examining themselves from its point

of view, they may become more convinced of the presence of sin in them, more humiliated on account of that sin, and hate sin the more.[12] Thus they gain a better awareness of their need for Christ and for the perfection of His obedience.[13] The prohibitions against sin[14] in the law are also useful in restraining believers from pursuing the desires of their old nature, and the punishments for disobedience in the law show them what their sins deserve and what afflictions they may expect for them in this life, even though they have been freed from the curse threatened in the law.[15] The promises of the law similarly show them that God approves obedience and that blessings may be expected for obedience,[16] although not as their due from the law as a covenant of works.[16a] The fact that the law encourages doing good and discourages doing evil does not mean that a person who does good and refrains from evil is under the law and not under grace.[17]

7. None of these uses of the law are contrary to the grace of the gospel. They rather beautifully comply with it,[18] because the Spirit of Christ subdues and enables the will of man to do voluntarily and cheerfully what the will of God, revealed in the law, requires to be done.[19]

Chapter 20

Concerning Christian Freedom and Freedom of Conscience

1. Christ has purchased for believers under the gospel freedom from the guilt of sin, from the condemning wrath of God, and from the curse of the moral law.[1] He has also freed them from the evil world we live in, from enslavement to Satan, from the dominion of sin,[2] the evil of afflictions, the sting of death, the victory of the grave, and from everlasting damnation.[3] In Christ believers have free access to God[4] and can obey Him, not out of slavish fear, but with a childlike love and a willing mind.[5] All these freedoms were also held by believers under the law.[6] However, under the New Testament, the liberty of Christians has been enlarged to include freedom from the yoke of the ceremonial law, to which the Jewish church was subjected.[7] Christians also have greater boldness of access to the throne of grace[8] and a fuller gift of the Spirit of God than believers ordinarily had under the law.[9]

2. God alone is Lord of the conscience and has left it free from the doctrines and commandments of men which are in any way contrary to or different from His word in matters of faith or worship.[10] And so, believing any such teachings or obeying any such commandments of men for conscience's sake actually betrays true freedom of conscience.[11] Requiring implicit or absolute, blind obedience also destroys freedom of conscience as well as the free use of reason.[12]

3. Those who practice any sin or nourish any sinful desire on the pretext of Christian freedom destroy the whole purpose of Christian freedom, which is, that, having been rescued out of the hands of our enemies, we might serve the Lord without fear and in holiness and righteousness before Him all the days of our lives.[13]

4. God intends that the authorities He has ordained on earth and the freedom Christ has purchased should not destroy but mutually uphold and preserve each other. And so, those who oppose any lawful power or the lawful exercise of power, whether civil or ecclesiastical, on the pretext of Christian freedom are actually resisting God.[14] The support, promotion, or practice of such opposition, which contradicts natural

understanding or the known principles of Christianity on matters of faith, worship, and associations, which denies the power of godliness, or which disrupts the peace and unity among believers, should lawfully be called to account and proceeded against by the church. [15/15a]

Chapter 21

Concerning Religious Worship and the Sabbath Day

1. Natural understanding reveals that there is a God, Who is Lord and sovereign over everything, Who is good and does good to everyone, and Who is therefore to be held in awe, loved, praised, called upon, trusted in, and served with all our heart, soul, and might.[1] The acceptable way of worshipping the true God is established by God Himself. God's revealed will so defines and outlines proper worship that neither the imaginations and devices of men nor the suggestions of Satan are to be followed. God is not to be worshipped under any visible representation or in any other way than that prescribed in Holy Scripture.[2]

2. Religious worship is to be given to God, the Father, Son, and Holy Spirit, and only to Him,[3] not to angels, saints, or any other creature.[4] Since the fall this worship must involve a mediator, and there is no other mediator than Christ alone.[5]

3. Prayer with thanksgiving is one part of religious worship[6] and is required by God from all men.[7] In order for prayer to be accepted, it must be made in the name of Jesus,[8] by the help of His Spirit,[9] according to His will,[10] with understanding, reverence, humility, fervor, faith, love, and perserverance,[11] and, if vocal, in a known tongue.[12]

4. Prayer is to be made for lawful things[13] and for people who are alive or may be born,[14] but not for the dead,[15] nor for those who are known to have committed the sin unto death.[16]

5. The ordinary worship of God includes: the reverent and attentive reading of the Scriptures;[17] the sound preaching[18] and conscientious hearing of the word in obedience to God with understanding and faith;[19] singing of psalms with grace in the heart;[20] and the proper administration and right receiving of the sacraments instituted by Christ.[21] Then there are religious oaths[22] and vows,[23] solemn fasting,[24] and thanksgiving on special occasions.[25] Worship should include these at appropriate times, and they should be performed in a holy and religious manner.[26]

6. Under the gospel neither prayer nor any other part of religious worship is tied to or made more acceptable by being performed in any particular place.[27] God is to be worshipped everywhere[28] in spirit and in truth:[29] in private families[30] daily;[31] privately by individuals daily;[32] and regularly in solemn public gatherings, which are not to be carelessly or willfully neglected or forsaken, since God calls us to join other believers in public worship.[33]

7. It is a law of our natural, earthly life that some appropriate amount of time be set aside for the worship of God. In His word God has similarly commanded all men in every age to keep one day in seven holy unto Him as a sabbath.[34] From the beginning of the world up to the resurrection of Christ this sabbath was the last day of the week. Since the resurrection of Christ it has been changed to the first day of the week, called the Lord's day in Scripture, and is to be continued until the end of the world as the Christian sabbath.[35]

8. The sabbath is kept holy unto the Lord when men: prepare their hearts for it; arrange for their daily affairs to be taken care of beforehand; rest the whole day from their own works and words, and from thoughts about their wordly activities and recreations;[36] and take up the whole time in public and private worship and in the duties of necessity and mercy.[37]

Chapter 22

Concerning Lawful Oaths and Vows

1. Lawful oaths are part of religious worship.[1] On proper occasions believers may solemnly swear and call God to witness that what they assert or promise is true, and they may ask God to judge them according to the truth or falsehood of what they swear.[2]

2. The name of God is the only name by which men should swear, and that name is to be used with holy awe and reverence.[3] Therefore to swear vainly or rashly by that glorious and mighty name or to swear at all by any other name is sinful and to be abhorred.[4] Just as in important matters an oath is warranted by the word of God, under the New as well as the Old Testament, so a lawful oath, required by legitimate authority in such matters ought to be taken.[5]

3. Whoever takes an oath ought to consider fully the importance of such a solemn act, and so he should swear to nothing but what he is completely convinced is true. No one may bind himself by an oath to anything but what is good and just, to what he believes to be true, and to what he is able and determined to perform. It is a sin to refuse to swear an oath about anything good and just, when it is required by lawful authority.[6]

4. An oath is to be taken in the plain, ordinary sense of the words used, without any equivocation or mental reservation.[7] It cannot obligate one to sin; but once taken about anything not sinful, it must be performed, even to one's own harm,[8] and must not be broken, even if made to heretics or atheists.[9]

5. A vow is similar to an oath promising something and should be made with similar religious care and performed with similar faithfulness.[10]

6. A vow should be made to no one but God.[11] In order to be accepted it should be made voluntarily in a faithful and conscientious way as thanks for mercy received or as a means of getting what we want. A vow binds us more strictly to necessary duties or to other things to such an extent and for as long as is appropriate.

7. No one may vow to do anything forbidden in the word of God, anything hindering a duty commanded in the word, or anything not in his own power, which he has neither the ability nor warrant from God to perform.[13] In this respect monastic vows of perpetual celibacy, professed poverty, and consistent obedience do not perfect us but are actually superstitious, sinful traps, in which no Christian should entangle himself. [13a]

Chapter 23

Concerning Civil Authorities

1. God, the supreme Lord and King of the whole world, has ordained civil authorities to be over people under Him for His own glory and the public good. For this purpose He has armed civil authorities with the power of the sword to defend and encourage those who are good and to punish wrongdoers.[1]

2. It is lawful for Christians to accept and execute offices of civil authority when that is their calling.[2] In the administration of such offices they should take care to support true religion, justice, and peace, according to the beneficial laws of each government,[3] and in so doing they may lawfully under the New Testament wage war on just and necessary occasions.[4]

3. Civil authorities may not take on themselves the ministering of God's word and the sacraments, the administration of spiritual power, or any interference with matters of faith.[5] Nevertheless it is the duty of civil authorities to protect the church of our Lord, without giving preference to any denomination of Christians, so that every person with church affiliations or duties will be able to function with complete and unquestioned freedom. Since Jesus Christ has directed the establishment of regular government and discipline in His church, no law of any civil government should interfere with, abridge, or hinder the proper exercise of church government among the voluntary members of Christian denominations, acting in accordance with their own professed beliefs. It is the duty of civil authorities to protect the person and good name of all people so that no one is abused, injured, or insulted on account of their religious faith or lack of it. [5a] It is also their duty to see to it that all religious and ecclesiastical assemblies are held without disturbance.[6]

4. It is people's duty to pray for those in authority,[7] to honor them,[8] to pay them taxes and whatever is owed them,[9] to obey their lawful commands, and to be subject to them for conscience's sake.[10] Unbelief or different religious views on the part of civil authorities does not mean

that they are to be disobeyed by believers, including clergymen,[12] in the legitimate pursuit of their duties.[11] The Pope, of course, has no power or jurisdiction over civil authorities or the people under them in secular affairs. The Pope never has any right to usurp secular authority, particularly capital punishment in cases of what is judged to be heresy or any other fault.[13]

Chapter 24

Concerning Marriage and Divorce

1. Marriage is to be between one man and one woman. It is not lawful for any man to have more than one wife, nor for any woman to have more than one husband at the same time.[1]

2. Marriage was ordained: for the mutual help of husband and wife;[2] for the legitimate propagation of mankind; for raising up a holy seed to the Church;[3] and for the prevention of moral impurity.[4]

3. All people who are mentally, emotionally, and physically capable may legally marry.[5] But it is the duty of Christians to marry only in the Lord. Therefore, those who profess the true reformed religion should not marry with infidels, papists, or other idolaters. The godly should not be unequally yoked in marriage with any who live a notoriously wicked life or who maintain damnable heresies.[6]

4. Marriage should not occur where the nearness of blood relationship is forbidden in the Bible.[7] Incestuous marriage can never be legitimized by any human law or consent of the parties involved.[8]

5. If adultery or fornication is discovered after a contractual commitment to marry has been made, but before the marriage itself, the innocent party has the right to dissolve the contract.[9] In the case of adultery after marriage, it is lawful for the innocent party to sue for divorce[10] and after the divorce to marry someone else, as if the guilty party were dead.[11]

6. Although the corrupt nature of man is inclined to support arguments for the wrong separation of those whom God has joined together in marriage, yet the only causes which warrant dissolving the bond of marriage are adultery or deliberate desertion which cannot be remedied in any way by the Church or civil authority.[12] Proceedings for divorce must be public and orderly, and the persons involved must not be allowed to manage their case according to their own desires and judgment.[13]

Chapter 24

Of Marriage and Divorce*

1. Christian marriage is an institution ordained of God, blessed by our Lord Jesus Christ, established and sanctified for the happiness and welfare of mankind, into which spiritual and physical union one man and one women enter, cherishing a mutual esteem and love, bearing with each other's infirmities and weaknesses, comforting each other in trouble, providing in honesty and industry for each other and for their household, praying for each other, and living together the length of their days as heirs of the grace of life.

2. Because the corruption of man is apt unduly to put asunder those whom God hath joined together in marriage, and because the Church is concerned with the establishment of marriage in the Lord as Scripture sets it forth, and with the present penitence as well as with the past innocence or guilt of those whose marriage has been broken; therefore as a breach of that holy relation may occasion divorce, so remarriage after a divorce granted on grounds explicitly stated in Scripture or implicit in the gospel of Christ may be sanctioned in keeping with his redemptive gospel, when sufficient penitence for sin and failure is evident, and a firm purpose of and endeavor after Christian marriage is manifest.

---

*(UP).

Chapter 24

Of Marriage and Divorce†

1. Marriage is a union between one man and one woman, designed of God to last so long as they both shall live.[1]

2. Marriage is designed for the mutual help of husband and wife;[2] for the safeguarding, undergirding, and development of their moral and spiritual character;[3] for the propagation of children and the rearing of them in the discipline and instruction of the Lord.[4]

3. All persons who are able with judgment to give their consent may marry,[5] except within the limits of blood relationship forbidden by Scripture,[6] and such marriages are valid before God in the eyes of the church.[7] But no marriage can be fully and securely Christian in spirit or in purpose unless both partners are committed to a common Christian faith and to a deeply shared intention of building a Christian home. Evangelical Christians should seek as partners in marriage only persons who hold in common a sound basis of evangelical faith.[8]

4. Marriage for the Christian has religious as well as civil significance.[9] The distinctive contribution of the church in performing the marriage ceremony is to affirm the divine institution of marriage;[10] to invoke God's blessing upon those who enter into the marital relationship in accordance with his word;[11] to hear the vows of those who desire to be married; and to assure the married partners of God's grace within their new relationship.[12]

5. It is the divine intention that persons entering the marriage covenant become inseparably united, thus allowing for no dissolution save that caused by the death of either husband or wife.[13] However, the weaknesses of one or both partners may lead to gross and persistent denial of the marriage vows so that marriage dies at the heart and the union becomes intolerable; yet only in cases of extreme, unrepented-of, and irremediable unfaithfulness (physical or spiritual) should separation or divorce be considered. Such separation or divorce is

†Chapter 26 (PC).

accepted as permissible only because of the failure of one or both of the partners, and does not lessen in any way the divine intention for indissoluble union.[14]

6. The remarriage of divorced persons may be sanctioned by the church, in keeping with the redemptive gospel of Christ, when sufficient penitence for sin and failure is evident, and a firm purpose of and endeavor after Christian marriage is manifested.[15]

7. Divorced persons should give prayerful thought to discover if God's vocation for them is to remain unmarried, since one failure in this realm raises serious question as to the rightness and wisdom of undertaking another union.[16]

Chapter 25

Concerning the Church

1. The catholic or universal church is invisible and consists of all the elect who have been, are, or ever will be gathered into one under Christ, the head. The church is His body and spouse, the fulness of God, Who fills all in all.[1]

2. The visible church is also catholic or universal under the gospel, i.e., it is not confined to one nation as previously under the Mosaic Law. It consists of everyone in the world who professes the true religion[2] together with their children.[3] The visible church is the kingdom of the Lord Jesus Christ[4] and the house and family of God,[5] outside of which people cannot ordinarily be saved.[6]

3. In order to gather and perfect the saints in this life until the end of the world Christ has given the ministry, Scriptures, and ordinances of God to this universal visible church, and by His own presence and Spirit He enables the church to function in this way according to His promise.[7]

4. This universal church has been sometimes more and sometimes less visible.[8] Particular churches, which are members of it, are also more or less pure, depending on how the gospel is accepted and taught, how the ordinances of God are administered, and how public worship is performed.[9]

5. The purest churches under heaven are subject both to impurity and error.[10] Some churches have so degenerated that they are not churches of Christ, but synagogues of Satan.[11] Nevertheless, there will always be a church on earth to worship God according to His will.[12]

6. There is no other head of the church than the Lord Jesus Christ.[13] In no sense can the Pope in Rome be the head of it. Rather, he is that Antichrist, the man of sin, and son of damnation, who glorifies himself as opposed to Christ and everything related to God.[13a]

Chapter 26

Concerning the Fellowship of the Saints

1. All believers are united to Jesus Christ, their head, by His Spirit and by faith, and have fellowship with Him in His grace, suffering, death, resurrection, and glory.[1] United to one another in love the saints have fellowship in each other's gifts and grace[2] and are obliged to perform those public and private duties which nourish their mutual good, both spiritually and physically.[3]

2. By their profession of faith saints are bound to maintain a holy fellowship and communion with each other in the worship of God and in the performance of other spiritual services for their mutual improvement.[4] They are also bound to help each other in material things according to their different abilities and needs. This fellowship is to be offered, as God gives the opportunity, to everyone in every place who calls on the name of the Lord Jesus.[5]

3. This communion which the saints have with Christ in no way means that they share in His Godhead or are equal with Him in any respect — to affirm either is impious and blasphemous.[6] Neither does their communion with each other take away or infringe the right each person has to own and possess goods and property.[7]

Chapter 27

Concerning the Sacraments

1. Sacraments are holy signs and seals of the covenant of grace. They were instituted by God along with that covenant[1] to represent Christ and His benefits, to confirm our position with and in Him,[2] to demonstrate a visible difference between those who belong to the church and the rest of the world,[3] and solemnly to engage believers in the service of God in Christ according to His word.[4]

2. In every sacrament there is a spiritual relationship or sacramental union between the sign and the thing signified. And so the names and effects of the one are attributed to the other.[5]

3. The grace revealed in or by sacraments in their right use does not come from any power in them. Neither does the effectiveness of a sacrament depend on the devoutness or the intention of whoever administers it. Rather the power and effectiveness of the sacraments are the result of the work of the Spirit[6] and rest on God's word instituting them, since His word authorizes their use and promises benefits to worthy receivers of them.[7]

4. There are only two sacraments ordained by Christ our Lord in the gospel: baptism and the Lord's supper.[8] Neither of these may be administered by anyone but a lawfully ordained minister of the word.[9]

5. The sacraments of the Old Testament signify and reveal in substance the same spiritual things as those of the New.[10]

Chapter 28

Concerning Baptism

1. Baptism is a sacrament of the New Testament, ordained by Jesus Christ.[1] By baptism a person is solemnly admitted into the visible church.[2] Baptism is also a sign and seal of the covenant of grace,[3] of the believer's ingrafting into Christ,[4] of rebirth,[5] of remission of sins,[6] and of the believer's yielding to God through Jesus Christ to walk in newness of life.[7] By Christ's own direction this sacrament is to be continued in His church until the end of the world.[8]

2. The physical substance to be used in this sacrament is water. The person is to be baptized in the name of the Father, the Son, and the Holy Spirit[9] by a lawfully called minister of the gospel.[10]

3. Dipping the person into the water is not necessary. Baptism is correctly administered by pouring or sprinkling water on the person.[11]

4. Not only those who actually profess faith in and obedience to Christ are to be baptized[12] but also the infants of one or both believing parents.[13]

5. Although it is a great sin to condemn or neglect this sacrament,[14] baptism is not inseparably connected with God's grace and salvation. One can be saved and reborn without baptism,[15] and, on the other hand, everyone who is baptized is not therefore unquestionably reborn.[16]

6. The effectiveness of baptism is not tied to that moment in time in which it is administered.[17] However, by the correct use of this sacrament the grace promised in it is not only offered but actually embodied and conferred by the Holy Spirit to everyone (adult or infant) to whom that grace is given, according to the purpose of God's own will and in His appointed time.[18]

7. The sacrament of baptism should be administered only once to a person.[19]

Chapter 29

Concerning the Lord's Supper

1. The night Jesus was betrayed He instituted the sacrament of His body and blood, called the Lord's supper, to be observed in His church until the end of the world as a perpetual remembrance of His sacrifice in death and as the seal of all the benefits of that sacrifice for true believers. It also signifies the spiritual nourishment and growth of believers in Jesus and their additional commitment to perform all the duties they owe Him. Finally it is a bond and pledge of believers' communion with Jesus and with each other as members of His mystical body.[1]

2. In this sacrament Christ is not offered up to His Father, nor is any actual sacrifice made for the remission of sins of the living or the dead.[1a] Rather this sacrament commemorates Christ's offering up of Himself, by Himself, on the cross once for all, and it spiritually offers up to God every possible praise for that sacrifice.[1b] Consequently the so-called sacrifice of the Roman Catholic mass does detestable injustice to Christ's one sacrifice, which is the only propitiation for all the sins of the elect.[2]

3. In the administration of the Lord's supper Jesus has directed His ministers to declare to the congregation His words instituting this sacrament, to pray, and to bless the bread and wine, which are thus set apart from their ordinary use and put to holy use. His ministers are to take and break the bread, to take the cup, and (communicating themselves, too) to give both to the communicants — but not to anyone else not present at that time in the congregation.[3/3a]

4. Practices contrary to the nature of this sacrament and to the institution of it by Christ are: private masses or receiving the sacrament alone from a priest or anyone else;[3b] denying the cup to the congregation;[3c] and worshipping the bread and wine themselves by lifting them up or carrying them around for adoration or reserving them for any counterfeit religious use.[4]

5. The bread and wine in this sacrament, properly set apart to the uses ordained by Christ, so relate to Him crucified that truly and yet only

sacramentally they are sometimes called by the name of what they represent, that is, the body and blood of Christ.[5] Even so, they still remain in substance and nature only bread and wine, as they were before their sacramental use.[6]

6. The teaching that the substance of the bread and wine is changed into the substance of Christ's body and blood (usually called transubstantiation) by the consecration of a priest or any other means is objectionable not only to Scripture but even to common sense and reason. Such teaching overturns the nature of the sacrament and has been and is the cause of much superstition and indeed flagrant idolatry.[7]

7. Worthy receivers, physically partaking of the visible substances of this sacrament, do then also by faith actually and in fact, but not physically or bodily, spiritually receive and feed on Christ crucified and on all the benefits of His death. The body and blood of Christ are not then bodily or physically in, with, or under the bread and wine; but they are actually spiritually present to the faith of believers in the administration of this sacrament, just as the bread and wine are physically present.[8]

8. Although ignorant or wicked men may partake of the physical substances in this sacrament, they do not receive what is signified by them. However, by their unworthy coming to the Lord's table they are guilty of His body and blood and damn themselves. Therefore, just as the ignorant and ungodly are not fit to enjoy communion with Christ, neither are they worthy to come to the Lord's table, and, as long as they remain ignorant and ungodly, they cannot and must not be allowed to partake of the holy mystery of communion without committing a great sin against Christ.[9]

Chapter 30

Concerning Condemnation by the Church

1. As king and head of His church, the Lord Jesus has directed the establishment of church government, separate from civil authority, which is to be administered by officers of the church.[1]

2. To these officers are committed the keys of the kingdom of heaven, which empower them: to free people from the guilt of sin or to bind them to it; to close the kingdom of heaven to the unrepentant by the word and condemnation; and to open the kingdom to repentant sinners by the ministry of the gospel and by withdrawing condemnation as the occasion demands.[2]

3. Condemnation by the church is necessary in order to reclaim and regain spiritual brothers who have committed some serious offense; to deter others from committing similar offenses; to purge that leaven which might contaminate the whole lump; to vindicate the honor of Christ and the holy profession of the gospel; and to avoid the wrath of God, which might justly fall on the church, should it allow His covenant and the sacraments to be profaned by notorious and obstinate offenders.[3]

4. The best way to accomplish these purposes is for the officers of the church to act in accordance with the severity of the offense and the guilt of the offender by: (1) warning the offender; (2) excluding him from the sacrament of the Lord's Supper for a time; or (3) excommunicating him from the church.[4]

Chapter 31

Concerning Synods and Councils

1. The assemblies which are generally called synods or councils ought to be held for the better government and continuing improvement of the church. By virtue of their office and the power Christ has given them to build up and not destroy, the leaders of particular churches should arrange for such assemblies and meet together in them as often as is judged necessary for the good of the church. [1/1a]

2. As far as the ministry is concerned, it is the responsibility of synods and councils: to settle controversies of faith and cases relating to matters of conscience; to set down rules and directions for the better administration of the public worship of God and of church government; and to hear complaints in cases of maladministration and authoritatively to settle them. If these decisions conform to the word of God, they are to be accepted reverently and submissively, not only because they agree with the word but also because they rest on authority ordained and arranged by God in His word. [2]

3. Since apostolic times all synods and councils, whether general or local, may make mistakes, and many have. Consequently synods and councils are not to be made a final authority in questions of faith and living but are to be used as an aid to both. [3]

4. Synods and councils should consider and settle only ecclesiastical questions. They are not to meddle in civil affairs which concern the state except in extraordinary cases of modest petitions or in an advisory capacity prompted by religious conscience, when requested by civil authorities. [4]

Chapter 32

Concerning the Condition of Man after Death and the Resurrection of the Dead

1. After death the bodies of human beings decompose and return to dust,[1] but their souls, which do not die or sleep, have an immortal existence and immediately return to God Who created them.[2] The souls of the righteous are then perfected in holiness and are received into the highest heavens, where they behold the face of God in light and glory and wait for the full redemption of their bodies.[3] The souls of the wicked are thrown into hell, where they remain in torment and complete darkness, set apart for the great day of judgment.[4] Scripture recognizes only these two places, and no other, for souls separated from their bodies.

2. Those who are alive at the last day will not die but will be changed.[5] At that time all the dead will be raised with the very same bodies and no other than the same bodies they had before, although with different characteristics, which will be united again to their souls forever.[6]

3. By the power of Christ the bodies of the unjust shall be raised to dishonor, but by His spirit the bodies of the just will be raised to honor and be made according to the pattern of His own glorious body.[7]

Chapter 33

Concerning the Last Judgment

1. God the Father has ordained a day in which He will judge the world in righteousness by Jesus Christ,[1] to Whom He has given all power and judgment.[2] In that day not only will the apostate angels be judged, but all the people who have lived on earth will appear before the court of Christ to give an account of their thoughts, words, and actions, and be judged according to what they have done in the body, whether good or evil.[3]

2. God's purpose in arranging for this day is to show forth the glory of His mercy in the eternal salvation of the elect[4] and the glory of His justice in the damnation of the reprobate, who are wicked and disobedient.[5] At that time the righteous will go into everlasting life and receive that fullness of joy and refreshment which will come from the presence of the Lord.[6] But the wicked, who do not know God and do not obey the gospel of Jesus Christ, will be thrown into eternal torment and punished with everlasting destruction away from the presence of the Lord and the glory of His power.[7]

3. Christ wants us to be completely convinced that there is going to be a day of judgment, as a deterrent to sin for everyone and as an added consolation for the godly in their suffering.[8] He has also made sure that no one knows when that day will be, so that we may never rest secure in our worldly surroundings, but, not knowing what hour the Lord will come, we must always be alert and may always be ready to say, "Come, Lord Jesus, come quickly."[9] Amen.

Chapter 34 *

Of the Holy Spirit

1. The Holy Spirit, the third person in the Trinity, proceeding from the Father and the Son, of the same substance and equal in power and glory, is, together with the Father and the Son, to be believed in, loved, obeyed, and worshipped throughout all ages.

2. He is the Lord and Giver of life, everywhere present, and is the source of all good thoughts, pure desires, and holy counsels in men. By him the prophets were moved to speak the word of God, and all the writers of the Holy Scriptures inspired to record infallibly the mind and will of God. The dispensation of the gospel is especially committed to him. He prepares the way for it, accompanies it with his persuasive power, and urges its message upon the reason and conscience of men, so that they who reject its merciful offer are not only without excuse, but are also guilty of resisting the Holy Spirit.

3. The Holy Spirit, whom the Father is ever willing to give to all who ask him, is the only efficient agent in the application of redemption. He regenerates men by his grace, convicts them of sin, moves them to repentance, and persuades and enables them to embrace Jesus Christ by faith. He unites all believers to Christ, dwells in them as their Comforter and Sanctifier, gives to them the spirit of Adoption and Prayer, and performs all these† gracious offices by which they are sanctified and sealed unto the day of redemption.

4. By the indwelling of the Holy Spirit all believers being vitally united to Christ, who is the Head, are thus united one to another in the church, which is his body. He calls and anoints ministers for their holy office, qualifies all other officers in the church for their special work, and imparts various gifts and graces to its members. He gives efficacy to the word and to the ordinances of the gospel. By him the church will be preserved, increased, purified, and at last made perfectly holy in the presence of God.

---

*Chapter 34 (UP), 9 (PC).

†. . . these (UP), those (PC).

Chapter 35[*]

Of the Gospel of the Love of God and Missions

1. God in infinite and perfect love, having provided in the covenant of grace, through the mediation and sacrifice of the Lord Jesus Christ, a way of life and salvation, sufficient for and adapted to the whole lost race of man, doth freely offer this salvation to all men in the gospel.

2. In the gospel God declares his love for the world and his desire that all men should be saved; reveals fully and clearly the only way of salvation; promises eternal life to all who truly repent and believe in Christ; invites and commands all to embrace the offered mercy; and by his Spirit accompanying the word pleads with men to accept his gracious invitation.

3. It is the duty and privilege of everyone who hears the gospel immediately to accept its merciful provisions; and they who continue in impenitence and unbelief incur aggravated guilt and perish by their own fault.

4. Since there is no other way of salvation than that revealed in the gospel, and since in the divinely established and ordinary method of grace faith cometh by hearing the word of God, Christ hath commissioned his church to go into all the world and to make disciples of all nations. All believers are, therefore, under obligation to sustain the ordinances of the Christian religion where they are already established, and to contribute by their prayers, gifts, and personal efforts to the extension of the kingdom of Christ throughout the whole earth.

---

*Chapter 35, Of the Gospel of the Love of God and Missions (UP); Chapter 10, Of the Gospel (PC).

Declaratory Statement *

While the ordination vow of ministers, ruling elders, and deacons, as set forth in the Form of Government, requires the reception and adoption of the Confession of Faith only as containing the system of doctrine taught in the Holy Scriptures, nevertheless, seeing that the desire has been formally expressed for a disavowal by the Church of certain inferences drawn from statements in the Confession of Faith, and also for a declaration of certain aspects of revealed truth which appear at the present time to call for more explicit statement, therefore The United Presbyterian Church in the United States of America does authoritatively declare as follows:

First, With reference to Chapter III of the Confession of Faith: that concerning those who are saved in Christ, the doctrine of God's eternal decree is held in harmony with the doctrine of his love to all mankind, his gift of his Son to be the propitiation for the sins of the whole world, and his readiness to bestow his saving grace on all who seek it; that concerning those who perish, the doctrine of God's eternal decree is held in harmony with the doctrine that God desires not the death of any sinner, but has provided in Christ a salvation sufficient for all, adapted to all, and freely offered in the gospel to all; that men are fully responsible for their treatment of God's gracious offer; that his decree hinders no man from accepting that offer; and that no man is condemned except on the ground of his sin.

Second, With reference to Chapter X, Section 3, of the Confession of Faith, that it is not to be regarded as teaching that any who die in infancy are lost. We believe that all dying in infancy are included in the election of grace, and are regenerated and saved by Christ through the Spirit, who works when and where and how he pleases.

---

*Additional interpretations of original Chapters 3 and 10 (UP).

Appendix I

Changes in the Text

The only substantive changes in the Westminster Confession of Faith as adopted by American Presbyterians in 1788 concerned statements about the relationship of secular government to the church. The original Confession of 1647 allows some secular authority and interference in church affairs, which the American Presbyterians were unwilling to grant. The great division of American Presbyterians in 1861 into the Presbyterian Church in the United States of America (PCUSA) and the Presbyterian Church in the United States (PCUS), did not create any fundamental changes in the text of the Confession up to 1902. Until then both used basically identical versions of the Confession (the basis of our modernized version). In 1903 PCUSA added two new chapters, "Of the Holy Spirit" (34) and "Of the Gospel of the Love of God and Missions" (35), and a "Declaratory Statement," interpreting the original Chapters 3 and 10. Later in this century PCUS added the same two chapters (without the declaratory statement) as new Chapters 9 ("Of the Holy Spirit") and 10 ("Of the Gospel") with only one minor verbal change ("these" to "those" in 9. 4). Original Chapter 9 ("Of Free Will") was renumbered 11 and the sequence followed down through 35. The only other major alteration to the original text has occurred in Chapter 24 (PCUS 26), "Of Marriage and Divorce." Both PCUSA and PCUS have rewritten this chapter, and so there are three versions of it in our text, both new versions after our modernization of the original chapter (which is identical to the 1647 chapter except for the clause in paragraph 3 forbidding marriage to a deceased wife's sister or husband's brother, a clause removed by both PCUSA and PCUS).

Listed below are all the other variations in the text prior to the 1902 American version and subsequent to it. In this list the different editions and versions are identified as follows: 1647 — the original British edition; AM — the 1902 version we have modernized; UP — the version currently used by UPCUSA; and PC — the version currently used by

PCUS. Our reference text for the 1647 text has been the copy in Philip Schaff, ed., *The Creeds of Christendom*, 4th ed. (New York: Harper, 1919), III, 600-673. For AM we have used the PCUS edition of 1910 (because it contains the 1910 changes to the proof texts), the PCUSA text of 1896, and the American edition of 1839. The last change to the PCUS text was proposed in 1962 and enacted in 1963. Consequently for PC we have used the revised 1963 edition of the Confession, which is the basis of the current paperback edition used by PCUS churches. PCUSA, of course, made their major changes to the Confession in 1903, and UPCUSA has adopted a new "Confession of 1967" which appears in their *Book of Confessions*, 2nd ed. (New York, 1970). We have referred to this edition's copy of the Westminster Confession and its 1903 additions. We have also checked and used UPCUSA or PCUSA texts of the Westminster Confession printed in their *Constitution* in 1959, 1958, 1954, 1953, and 1924.

Variants are listed by chapter and paragraph with the AM reading first followed by a semicolon and other readings.

1. 2. The Revelation] AM, UP; The Revelation of John 1647; Revelation PC
    5. esteem for the Holy Scripture] AM, PC; esteem of the Holy Scripture 1647, UP
    6. and that there are] AM, PC; and there are 1647, UP
    8. into the vulgar language of every nation] AM, 1647, UP; into the language of every people PC
    9. it may be searched] AM, UP, PC; it must be searched 1647

3. Of God's Eternal Decrees] AM, PC; Of God's Eternal Decree 1647, UP
    5. of his mere free grace and love] AM, 1647; of his free grace and love alone UP, PC

5. 5. support upon himself] AM, UP, PC; support unto himself 1647

9(11). 1. that it is neither] AM, UP, PC; that is neither 1647
        to good or evil] AM, UP, PC; to do good or evil 1647
        2. which is good] AM, UP, PC; which was good 1647

10(12). 4. and maintain that they may is very pernicious, and to be detested] AM, 1647; and maintain that they may is without warrant of the word of God UP, PC

58

11(13).   1.   not by imputing] AM, UP, PC; nor by imputing 1647

16(18).   4.   requires, that] AM, UP, PC; requires, as that 1647

7.   Works done by unregenerate men, although for the matter of them they may be things which God commands, and of good use both to themselves and others; yet because they proceed not from a heart purified by faith; nor are done in a right manner, according to the word; nor to a right end, the glory of God; they are therefore sinful, and cannot please God, or make a man meet to receive grace from God. And yet their neglect of them is more sinful, and displeasing unto God.] AM, 1647, PC; Works done by unregenerate men, although for the matter of them they may be things which God commands, and in themselves praiseworthy and useful, and although the neglect of such things is sinful and displeasing unto God; yet, because they proceed not from a heart purified by faith; nor are done in a right manner, according to his Word; nor to a right end, the glory of God; they come short of what God requires, and do not make any man meet to receive the grace of God. UP

20(22).   1.   and a willing mind] AM, UP, PC; and willing mind 1647
              fuller communications] AM, PC; full communications 1647, UP

2.   commandments] AM, UP, PC; commands 1647
      the requiring an] AM, PC; the requiring of 1647, UP

4.   powers which God] AM, UP, PC; power which God 1647
      censures of the church] AM, UP, PC; censures of the church, and by the power of the civil magistrate 1647

21(23).   1.   limited by] AM, UP, PC; limited to 1647
              representation] AM, UP, PC; representations 1647

4.   not for the dead, nor for those of whom it may be known that they have sinned the sin unto death] AM, 1647; not for the dead UP, PC

5.   oaths, and vows] AM, UP, PC; oaths, vows 1647
      special occasions] AM, UP; several occasions 1647;

special occasion PC

6. spirit and in truth] AM, UP, PC; spirit and truth 1647

22(24). 3. perform. Yet it is a sin to refuse an oath touching anything that is good and just, being imposed by lawful authority.] AM, 1647, PC; perform UP

6. for obtaining] AM, UP, PC; for the obtaining 1647

7. which respects, popish monastical] AM; which respect, popish monastical 1647; which respects, monastical UP, PC

23(25). 2. just and necessary occasions] AM, UP, PC: just and necessary occasion 1647

3. Civil magistrates may not assume to themselves the administration of the word and sacraments; or the power of the keys of the kingdom of heaven; or, in the least, interfere in matters of faith. Yet, as nursing fathers, it is the duty of civil magistrates to protect the church of our common Lord, without giving the preference to any denomination of Christians above the rest, in such a manner that all ecclesiastical persons whatever shall enjoy the full, free, and unquestioned liberty of discharging every part of their sacred functions, without violence or danger. And, as Jesus Christ hath appointed a regular government and discipline in his church, no law of any commonwealth should interfere with, let, or hinder, the due exercise thereof, among the voluntary members of any denomination of Christians, according to their own profession and belief. It is the duty of civil magistrates to protect the person and good name of all their people, in such an effectual manner as that no person be suffered, either upon pretense of religion or infidelity, to offer any indignity, violence, abuse, or injury to any other person whatsoever: and to take order, that all religious and ecclesiastical assemblies be held without molestation or disturbance.] AM, UP, PC; The civil magistrate may not assume to himself the administration of the Word and Sacraments, or the power of the keys of the kingdom of heaven: yet he hath authority, and it is his duty to take order, that unity and peace be preserved in the Church, that the truth of God be kept pure and entire, that all blasphemies and heresies be suppressed, all corruptions

60

and abuses in worship and discipline prevented or reformed, and all the ordinances of God duly settled, administered, and observed. For the better effecting whereof he hath power to call synods, to be present at them, and to provide that whatsoever is transacted in them be according to the mind of God. 1647

4.   duty of the people] AM, PC; duty of people 1647, UP
   any power or jurisdiction] AM, UP, PC; any power and jurisdiction 1647

24.   4.   as man and wife.] UP *and* PC *before 1903 and subsequent twentieth-century revisions;* as man and wife. The man may not marry any of his wife's kindred nearer in blood than he may of his own, nor the woman of her husband's kindred nearer in blood than of her own. 1647 *and* AM *before the split into P-CUSA and PCUS.*

25(27). 2.   together with their children] AM, UP, PC; and of their children 1647
   out of which there is no ordinary possibility of salvation] AM, 1647; through which men are ordinarily saved, and union with which is essential to their best growth and service UP, PC

5.   as to become no churches of Christ, but synagogues of Satan] AM, 1647; as to become apparently no churches of Christ UP, PC

6.   There is no other head of the Church but the Lord Jesus Christ: nor can the Pope of Rome, in any sense be head thereof; but is that Antichrist, that man of sin and son of perdition, that exalteth himself in the Church against Christ, and all that is called God] AM, 1647; The Lord Jesus Christ is the only head of the Church, and the claim of any man to be the vicar of Christ and the head of the Church is unscriptural, without warrant in fact, and is a usurpation dishonoring to the Lord Jesus Christ UP; The Lord Jesus Christ is the only head of the church, and the claim of any man to be the vicar of Christ and the head of the church, is without warrant in fact or in Scripture, even anti-Christian, a usurpation dishonoring to the Lord Jesus Christ PC

26(28). 1. All saints that are united] AM, 1647, UP; All saints being united PC
2. saints by profession] AM, 1647, UP; saints by their profession PC
3. property] AM, UP, PC; propriety 1647

27(29). 2. and effects] AM, UP, PC; and the effects 1647

29(31). 2. but only a commemoration of that one offering up of himself, by himself, upon the cross, once for all, and a spiritual oblation of all possible praise unto God for the same; so that the popish sacrifice of the mass, as they call it, is most abominably injurious to Christ's one only sacrifice, the alone propitiation for all the sins of the elect] AM, 1647; but a commemoration of that one offering up of himself, by himself, upon the cross, once for all, and a spiritual oblation of all possible praise unto God for the same; so that the so-called sacrifice of the mass is most contradictory to Christ's one sacrifice, the only propitiation for all the sins of the elect UP, PC
3. to give both to the communicants but to none who are not then present in the congregation] AM, 1647, UP; to give both to the communicants PC
8. body and blood of the Lord, to their own damnation. Wherefore all ignorant and ungodly persons, as they are unfit to enjoy communion with him, so are they unworthy of the Lord's table, and can not, without great sin against Christ, while they remain such, partake of these holy mysteries, or be admitted thereunto] AM, 1647; body and blood of the Lord, and bring judgment on themselves. Wherefore all ignorant and ungodly persons, as they are unfit to enjoy communion with him, so are they unworthy of the Lord's Table, and cannot, without great sin against Christ, while they remain such, partake of these holy mysteries, or be admitted thereunto UP; body and blood of the Lord, and bring judgment on themselves PC

30(32). 3. from like offenses] AM, UP, PC; from the like offenses 1647

31(33). 1. commonly called synods or councils: and it belongeth to the overseers and other rulers of the particular churches, by virtue of their office, and the power which Christ hath given them for edification, and not for destruction, to appoint such assemblies; and to convene together in them, as often as they shall judge it expedient for the good of the church] AM, UP, PC; commonly called synods or councils 1647

2. *The following paragraph was omitted entirely from AM (and subsequent UP and PC). Then the original 1647 paragraphs 3-5 were renumbered 2-4:*
As magistrates may lawfully call a synod of ministers and other fit persons to consult and advise with about matters of religion; so if magistrates be open enemies to the Church, the ministers of Christ, of themselves by virtue of their office, or they, with other fit persons, upon delegation from their churches, may meet together in such assemblies. 1647

32(34). State of Man] AM, UP, PC; State of Men 1647

In 1903 the following was inserted between chapter 33 and new chapter 34 in UP; it was subsequently dropped:

PREAMBLE TO NEW CHAPTERS

Whereas, It is desirable to express more fully the doctrine of the Church concerning the Holy Spirit, missions, and the love of God for all men, the following chapters are added to the Confession of Faith:

Appendix II

Changes in the Proof Texts

The first version of the Westminster Confession which was presented to the English Parliament late in 1646 consisted only of the text itself. Parliament, however, demanded that the doctrinal positions articulated in the Confession be supported by specific passages from the Bible. The Westminster Assembly agreed, of course, and so the authorized edition of 1647 has proof texts. Very minor additions and deletions seem to have been made from then on in the English and Scottish editions. The first American edition of 1797 also made some alterations to the proof texts. These are included in Schaff's text (4th ed.), which is the basis for our text and proof texts. As the American text went through various editions, it accumulated a number of changes (particularly in 1821 and 1833). We compared the original proof texts in Schaff to the 1839 American edition and found that the proof texts to some chapters had been changed by five to ten percent. The major American changes to the proof texts, however, came after the church split in 1861. In 1894 PCUSA approved a complete revision of their proof texts, and subsequently in 1910 PCUS adopted and published an even more extensive revision. In preparing the text of the Confession for the proposed union of PCUSA with the United Presbyterian Church of North America (a union accomplished in 1958 creating the current UPCUSA) all proof texts were dropped. Consequently the Constitutions for UPCUSA of 1958, 1959 and following years have only the text of the Confession, while the PCUSA editions of 1954 and earlier have both.

We found it impossible to keep track of all the minor changes to the proof texts in British and American editions. What we have listed below are (1) the proof texts in the original 1647 British edition with the original American modifications of 1797, along with (2) all the changes made by PCUSA in their major 1894 revision and (3) all the changes made by PCUS in 1910. These revisions basically represent the proof texts as they now stand, for which the original British and American proof texts provide an interesting and significant context.

For the sake of space and appearance Scriptural references are not quoted, but only cited by book, chapter, and verse. We have adopted a simple system of notation so that the reader can immediately and readily recognize the status of any particular proof text or of the whole annotation to any paragraph or chapter. Scripture references which remain unchanged from the 1647 edition to the current PCUS edition and the last PCUSA edition are not distinguished in any way. References which appear in the original edition but which have subsequently been deleted are: (1) for PCUSA enclosed in inverted brackets, thus —]John 10:2[; and (2) for PCUS enclosed in inverted parentheses, thus —)John 10:2(. If the original reference has been deleted in both PCUSA and PCUS revisions, then the citation is enclosed in inverted brackets and parentheses, thus —])John 10:2([. We have used Schaff's edition for these original proof texts and have also included proof texts added in the 1797 American edition. These early American additions are italicized. References which appear in the revised PCUSA text but not in the original are enclosed in normal brackets, thus — [John 8:10]. References in the revised PCUS edition but not in the original are similarly enclosed in normal parentheses, thus — (John 8:10). If both PCUSA and PCUS editions have added the same new reference, it is enclosed in brackets and parentheses, thus — [(John 8:10)].

Since only the PCUS has retained proof texts, we have used their system of notation by arabic numerals beginning (with a few exceptions) at "1" for each chapter and numbering consecutively. For the sake of comparison we have also listed the PCUSA notation by letter, beginning with "a" and proceding consecutively for each chapter. This notation appears beside the appropriate PCUS number in the left margin. In cases where a whole note has disappeared in the modern revisions, we have added it in the appropriate place. These notes are distinguished by the addition of a letter, beginning with "a" to the immediately previous note (e.g. 6a), or, if the deleted note precedes the revised first note in a chapter, to note 1 (1a). Although there are three texts of Chapter 24 on marriage, there are only two sets of proof texts: (1) the proof texts for the original chapter as modified by PCUSA and PCUS; and (2) a new set of proof texts for the new PCUS chapter. The 1953 revision of Chapter 24 by PCUSA did not include proof texts.

Chapter 1

(General Note: At several points the Confession of Faith is more specific in its statements than the Scriptures. These statements are inferences drawn from the Scriptures or from statements based on the Scriptures, or from the experience and observation of the Church. In such cases, no texts are cited, but reference is made to this General Note.)

a	1.	Rom 2:14,15; Rom 1:19,20;)Psa 19:1-3, ([4]; Rom 1:32;)Rom 2:1(.
b	2.	I Cor 1:21; I Cor 2:13,14; (I Cor 2:9-12; Acts 4:12; Rom 10:13,14).
c	3.	Heb 1:1, [(2)]; (Gal 1:11,12; Deut 4:12-14).
d	4.	)]Prov 22:19-21[; Luke 1:3,4(; Rom 15:4;) Matt 4:4,7,10; Isa 8:]19[, 20(; (Luke 24:27; II Tim 3:16; II Pet 3:15, 16).
e	5.	II Tim 3:15,(16); II Pet 1:10; (Luke 16:29-31; Heb 2:1-3).
f	6.	)Heb 1:1,2(; (see General Note).
g	6a.	])Luke 16:29,31[; Eph 2:20; Rev 22:18,19; II Tim 3:16(; [Matt 11:27].
h	7.	)Luke 24:27,44; Rom 3:2; II Pet 1:21(. (The Canon of Scripture is not established by explicit passages, but by the testimony of Jesus and His apostles; of ancient manuscripts and versions; of ancient Christian writers and church councils, and by the internal evidence exhibited in the separate books.)
j	8.	]II Pet 1:)19(, 21[; II Tim 3:16;)I John 5:9(; I Thess 2:13; (Gal 1:11,12).
k,l	9.	)I Tim 3:15; I John 2:20,27(; John 16:13,14; I Cor 2:10, 11,)12(;])Isa 59:21([; (I Cor 2:6-9).
	10.	(Mark 7:5-7).
m	11.	)II Tim 3:15-17; Gal 1:8,]9[; II Thess 2:2(. (This statement is an inference from the sufficiency of the Scriptures.)
n	12.	John 6:45; I Cor 2:9,10,12.
o	13.	I Cor 11:13,14; I Cor 14:26,40.
p	14.	II Pet 3:16; (John 16:17; John 6:60).
q	15.	Psa 119:105,130; ([Acts 17:11],12).
	16.	(See note under Section 3, Figure 7 above.)
r,s	17.	)Matt 5:18(; Isa 8:20; Acts 15: (14),15,(16-18);)John 5:]39[,46(.

t	18.	]John 5:39[; ([II Tim 3:14,15]; II Pet 1:19); [Acts 17:11].
u,w,x	19.	I Cor 14:6,9,11,12,24,27,28; Col 3:16; Rom 15:4; (Matt 28:19,20).
y	20.	)II Pet 1:20,21; Acts 15:15; *John 5:46*(; (Matt 4:5-7; Matt 12:1-7).
z	21.	Matt 22:29,31;])Eph 2:20([; Acts 28:25; (Luke 10:26); [Gal 1:10; I John 4:1-6].

Chapter 2

a,b	1.	Deut 6:4; I Cor 8:4,6; I Thess 1:9; Jer 10:10.
c	2.	)Job 11:7,8,9; Job 26:14(; (Jer 23:24; Psa 147:5; I Kings 8:27; Psa 139).
d	3.	John 4:24.
e	4.	I Tim 1:17.
f,g	5.	Deut 4:15,16;)John 4:24(; Luke 24:39;)Acts 14:11,15(.
h	6.	James 1:17; Mal 3:6.
i	7.	I Kings 8:27; Jer 23:23,24.
k	8.	Psa 90:2; I Tim 1:17.
l	9.	Psa 145:3; (Rom 11:33).
m	10.	)Gen 17:1(; Rev 4:8.
n	11.	Rom 16:27.
o	12.	Isa 6:3; Rev 4:8.
p	13.	Psa 115:3.
q	14.	)Exod 3:14(; (Isa 44:6; Acts 17:24,25).
r	15.	Eph 1:11.
s	16.	)Prov 16:4(; Rom 11:36; Rev 4:11.
t	17.	I John 4:8, (9,10),)16(; [John 3:16].
u	18.	Exod 34:6,7.
w	19.	Heb 11:6.
x	20.	Neh 9:32,33; [Heb 10:28-31].
y	21.	Psa 5:5,6; (Hab 1:13).
z	22.	Nahum 1:2,3; Exod 34:7.
a,b,c,d	23.	John 5:26; Acts 7:2; Psa 119:68; I Tim 6:15; Rom 9:5.
e,f	24.	Acts 17:24,25;])Job 22:2,23([; [Ps 50:12; Isa 4:12-17].
g	25.	Rom 11:36; (Isa 40:12-17).
h	26.	)Rev 4:11; I Tim 6:15(; Dan 4:25,)35(; (Eph 1:11).
i	27.	Heb 4:13.
k	28.	Rom 11:33,34; Psa 147:5.
l	29.	Acts 15:18;]Ezek 11:5[; (Isa 46:9-11); [Prov 15:3].
m	30.	Psa 145:17; Rom 7:12.
n	31.	Rev 5:12-14; (Rev 7:11,12).

o   32.   ])I John 5:7([; Matt 3:16,17; Mat 28:19; II Cor 13:14; [Eph 2:18].

p   33.   John 1:14,18; (John 17:24); [Heb 1:2-6; Col 1:15-17].

q   34.   John 15:26; Gal 4:6.

Chapter 3

a   1.   Eph 1:11;)Rom 11:33; Heb 6:17;]Rom 9:15,18[(; (Acts 4:27,28; Matt 10:29,30; Eph 2:10); [Isa 45:6,7].

b   2.   James 1:13,[14],])17([; I John 1:5;])*Eccl 7:29*([; [Psa 5:4].

c   3.   Acts 2:23; Matt 17:12; Acts 4:27,28; John 19:11;]Prov 16:33[; ([Acts 27:23,24,34],44).

d   4.   )Acts 15:18(; I Sam 23:11,12; Matt 11:21,23; (Psa 139: 1-4): [Prov 16:33].

e   5.   Rom 9:11,13,[15],16,18; (II Tim 1:9; Eph 1:4,5).

f   6.   I Tim 5:21;)Matt 25:[31],41(; (Acts 13:48; Rom 8:29,30; John 10:27-29); [Mark 8:38; Jude 6].

g   7.   Rom 9:22,23;)Eph 1:5,6; Prov 16:4(; (Matt 25:41; Jude 4).

h   8.   II Tim 2:19; John 13:18; ([John 10:14-16, 27,28],29; John 6:37-39; Acts 13:48); [John 17:2,6,9-12].

i   9.   Eph 1:4.

       10.   Eph 1:11.

       11.   Eph 1:9.

       12.   II Tim 1:9.

       13.   Rom 8:30;)I Thess 5:9(; (I Pet 5:10).

k   14.   )Rom 9:11,13,[15],16(; Eph 1:])4([, (6),)9(; (II Tim 1:9; [Eph 2:8,9]).

l   15.   Eph 1:(5),6,12.

m   16.   I Pet 1:2; Eph 1:4,])5([; Eph 2:10; II Thess 2:13.

n   17.   I Thess 5:9,10; Tit 2:14; (Rom 5:19).

       18.   (Rom 9:11; II Thess 2:13,14; I Cor 1:9).

o   19.   Rom 8:30.

       20.   Eph 1:5.

       21.   II Thess 2:13; (Eph 1:4; I Thess 4:3).

p   22.   I Pet 1:5; (John 10:28).

q   23.   John 17:9;)Rom 8:28]-39[(; John 6:64,65; John 8:47; John 10:26; I John 2:19; (Acts 13:48).

r   24.   Matt 11:25,26;)I Pet 2:8(.

       25.   Rom 9:(14-16), 17,18,(19,20),21,22;)Jude 4(; (Rom 2: 8,9; II Thess 2:10-12).

	26.	)II Tim 2:]19[,20(; (Rev 15:3,4).
s,t,u,w	27.	)Rom 9:20; Rom 11:33; Deut 29:29; II Pet 1:10; Eph 1:6; Rom 11:5,6,20; Rom 8:33; Luke 10:20(; (see General Note).

Chapter 4

a	1a.	Heb 1:2; John 1:2,3; Gen 1:(1),2,(3);])Job 26:13; Job 33: 4([; [Rom 11:36; I Cor 8:6].
b	1b.	)Rom 1:20(; Jer 10:12; Psa 104:24;])Psa 33:5,6([.
c	1.	Gen 1;]Heb 11:3[; Col 1:16;)Acts 17:24(; [(Exod 20: 11)].
d	2.	Gen 1:27.
e	3.	)Gen 2:7; Eccles 12:7(;]Luke 23:43[; Matt 10:28; ([Psa 8:5],6; Gen 2:19,20).
f	4.	Gen 1:26;]Col 3:10; Eph 4:24[.
g	5.	Rom 2:14,15.
h,i	6.	])Eccles 7:29([; Gen 3:6, (17); (Gen 2:16,17); [Col 3:10; Eph 4:24].
k	7.	(Gen 2:16,[17]).
	8.	Gen 2:17; Gen 3:]8-11, 23[.
l	9.	Gen 1:])26([,28; *Psa 8:6-8;* [Gen 1:29,30].

Chapter 5

a,b,c,	1.	]Heb 1:3[;)Dan 4:34,35(; Psa 135:6; Acts 17:25,)26(,]28[;]Job 38-41[; Matt 10:29-31; *Matt 6:26,30;* [(Neh 9: 6); Psa 114:14-16].
d	2.	Prov 15:3; *II Chron 16:9;* Psa 104:24;]Psa 145:17[.
e	3.	Acts 15:18;)Psa 94:8-11(.
f	4.	Eph 1:11; Psa 33:)10(,11.
g	5.	])Isa 63:14([; Eph 3:10; Rom 9:17;)Gen 45:7(; Psa 145:)7(.
h	6.	Acts 2:23; (see under figures 3 and 4 above); [Jer 32:19].
i	7.	Gen 8:22; Jer 31:35.
	8.	]Exod 21:13;)Deut 19:5(; I Kings 22:)28(,34[; Isa 10:6,7; (Gen 50:19,20).
k	9.	Acts 27:[(24)],31,]44[; Isa 55:10,11;])Hos 2:21,22([.
l	10.	Hos 1:7;])Matt 4:4; Job 34:10([.
m	11.	Rom 4:]19[,20,21.

n	12.	]II Kings 6:6[; Dan 3:27; [I Kings 18:17-39; John 11:43-45; Rom 1:4].
	13.	(This statement is sustained by the doctrines of God's decrees and providence. See citations under Chapter 3 and Chapter 5, Sections 1,2,3.)
o	14.	Rom 11:32,33,)34(;]II Sam 24:1;)I Chron 21:1; I Kings 22:22,23; I Chron 10:4,13,14; II Sam 16:10; Acts 2:23([; Acts 4:27,28; (see citations under Chapter 3 and Chapter 5, Sections 1,2,3); [Isa 45:7].
p	15.	)Acts 14:16; Psa 76:10(; II Kings 19:28; (Isa 10:5-7,12, 15).
q	16.	Gen 50:20;)Isa 10:]6,7[,12(,[13-15]; (see under figure 15 above).
r	17.	James 1:]13,14[,)17(; I John 2:16; Psa 50:21.
s	18.	II Chron 32:25,26,31;)II Sam 24:1,[25](;(Deut 8:2); [Luke 22:31,32].
t	19.	II Cor 12:7-9; Psa 73; Psa 77:1-10,(11),12; Mark 14:66-72; John 21:15-17, [18-19].
u	20.	Rom 1:24,[25],]26[,28; Rom 11:7,8; (II Thess 2:11,12).
w	21.	Deut 29:4; [(Mark 4:11,12)].
x	22.	Matt 13:12; Matt 25:29; [Acts 13:10,11; II Cor 11:13,15].
y	23.	])Deut 2:30([; II Kings 8:12,13.
z	24.	Psa 81:11,12; II Thess 2:10-12; [II Cor 2:11; II Cor 11:3].
a	25.	Exod 7:3; Exod 8:15,32; II Cor 2:15,16; Isa 8:14; I Pet 2:7,8; Isa 6:9,10; Acts 28:26,27.
b	26.	)I Tim 4:10(; Amos 9:8,9; Rom 8:28;])Isa 43:3-5,14([; (Eph 1:22); [Matt 16:18].

Chapter 6

a	1.	Gen 3:13; II Cor 11:3; (Gen 3:1-14).
b	2.	)Rom 11:32(; (Rom 5:19,[20,21]).
c	3.	Gen 3:)6(,7,8;)]Eccles 7:29[; Rom 3:23(; (Gen 2:17).
d	4.	)Gen 2:17; Eph 2:1,[2,3](; *Rom 5:12;* (Eph 2:3).
e	5.	)Tit 1:15(; Gen 6:5; Jer 17:9; Rom 3:10-18,]19[; (Rom 8:6-8; Psa 58:1-5).
f	6.	])Gen 1:27,28([; Gen 2:]16[,17; Rom 5:12,15-19; Acts 17:26; I Cor 15:21,22,45,49.
g	7.	Psa 51:5; Gen 5:3;])Job 14:4; Job 15:14([; ([John 3,6]; Rom 3:10-18).
h,i	8.	Rom 5:6; Rom 7:18; Rom 8:7;)Col 1:21(;]*John 3:6*[;

)Gen 6:5(; Gen 8:21; Rom 3:10-12(13-19) — *by a misprint, this last entry does not appear in the latest edition of PC.*

k	9.	James 1:14,15;)Eph 2:2,3(; Matt 15:19.
l	10.	I John 1:8,10; Rom 7:14,17,18,[21,22],23; James 3:2; Prov 20:9;)Eccles 7:20(.
m	11.	Rom 7:]5[,7,8,25;)Gal 5:17(.
n,o	12.	I John 3:4; Rom 2:15; Rom 3:)9(, 19.
p	13.	Eph 2:3; (Rom 5:12).
q	14.	Gal 3:10.
r	15.	Rom 6:23; (Gen 2:17).
s,t,u	16.	Eph 4:18;)]Rom 8:20[;Lam 3:39(; Matt 25:41; II Thess 1:9; ₍Rom 1:21-28; Lev 26:14ff; Deut 28:15ff).

Chapter 7

a	1.	)]Isa 40:13-17[; Job 9:32,33;]I Sam 2:25; Psa 100:2,3[; Psa 113:5,6;]]Job 22:2,3[; Job 35:7,8; Luke 17:10; Acts 17:24,25(; (see General Note).
b	2.	]*Hos 6:7*[; *Gen 2:16,17;* Gal 3:10; (Rom 5:12,19; I Cor 15:22,47); [Gal 3:12].
c	2a.	)Rom 5:12-14,]15-20[; Rom 10:5(.
d	3.	)Gen 2:17; Gal 3:10;(((Compare Gen 2:16,17 with Rom 5:12-14; Rom 10:5; Luke 10:25-28; and with the covenants made with Noah and Abraham.)
e	4.	Gal 3:21;)Rom 3:20,21(; Rom 8:3; Gen 3:15; Isa 42:6; (Matt 26:28; Heb 10:5-10).
f	5.	])Mark 16:15,16([; John 3:16;)Rom 10:6,9;]Gal 3:11[(; (Acts 16:30,31); [Matt 28:18-20; Rom 1:16,17].
g	6.	Ezek 36:26,27; John 6:[(37)],44,)45(;])*John 5:37*([; (John 3:5-8); [Acts 13:48; Luke 11:13; Gal 3:14].
h	6a.	)Heb 9:15-17;]Heb 7:22; Luke 22:20; I Cor 11:25[(.
i	7.	II Cor 3:6-9; (Heb 1:1,2).
k	8.	Heb 8,9,10; Rom 4:11;)Col 2:11,12; I Cor 5:7;]*Col 2: 17*[(.
l	9.	)I Cor 10:1-4(; Heb 11:13; John 8:56; (Gal 3:6-8).
m	10.	Gal 3:)7(,8,9,14; (Acts 15:11; Rom 3:30).
n	10a.	)]Gal 2:17[; *Col 2:17*(.
o	11.	Matt 28:19,20; I Cor 11:23-25;])*II Cor 3:7-11*([.
p	12.	)Heb 12:22-25,]25-28[; Jer 31:33,34(; (Heb 8:6-13; [II Cor 3:9-11]).

q	13.	])Matt 28:19([; Eph 2:15-19; (see under figure 11 above); [Luke 2:32; Acts 10:34,35].
r,s	14.	)Luke 22:20;]*Heb 8:7-9*[; Gal 3:14,16; Acts 15:11; Rom 3:21,22,]23[,30;]Psa 32:1[; Rom 4:]3,6[,16,17,23, 24;]Heb 13:8[(; (Gal 3:17,29; see context and citations under figure 10 above); '[Heb 1:1,2].

Chapter 8

a	1.	Isa 42:1; I Peter 1:19,20; John 3:16; I Tim 2:5.
b	2.	Acts 3:[20-21],22; *Deut 18:15*.
c	3.	Heb 5:5,6.
d	4.	Psa 2:6; Luke 1:33; [(Isa 9:6,7)].
e	5.	Eph 5:23.
f	6.	Heb 1:2.
g	7.	Acts 17:31; [(II Cor 5:10)].
h	8.	John 17:6;)Psa 22:30(; Isa 53:10; ([Eph 1:4]; John 6:37, 39).
i	9.	I Tim 2:[(5)],6;)Isa 55:4,5(; I Cor 1:30; (Mark 10:45; [Rom 8:30]).
k	10.	John 1:1,14; I John 5:20; Phil 2:6; Gal 4:4; (Heb 2:14).
l	11.	Heb 2:)14,]16[(,17; Heb 4:15.
m	12.	Luke 1:27,31,35; Gal 4:4; (see under figure 10 above).
n	13.	)Luke 1:35(; Col 2:9; Rom 9:5;])I Pet 3:18; I Tim 3:16([; [Matt 16:16]; (see under figure 12 above).
o	14.	Rom 1:3,4; I Tim 2:5.
p	15.	)Psa 45:7; John 3:34(; (Luke 4:18,19,21; Acts 10:38); [Heb 1:8,9].
q	16.	Col 2:3.
r	17.	Col 1:19.
s,t	18.	Heb 7:26; John 1:14;)Acts 10:38; Heb 12:24; Heb 7:22(; (Luke 4:18-21).
u	19.	Heb 5:4,5.
w	20.	John 5:22,27; Matt 28:18;])Acts 2:36([.
x	21.	Psa 40:7,8;)Heb 10:5-10;]John 10:18[(; Phil 2:(5-7),8; [John 4:34].
y	22.	Gal 4:4.
z	23.	Matt 3:15;)Matt 5:17(; (John 17:4).
a	24.	Matt 26:37,38; Luke 22:44; Matt 27:46.
b	25.	Matt 26 and 27.
c	26.	Phil 2:8.

d	27.	Acts 2:])23([,24,27; Acts 13:37;)Rom 6:9(; [Matt 27:60].
e	28.	I Cor 15:])3([,4.
f	29.	John 20:25,27.
g	30.	])Mark 16:19([; ([Luke 24:50,51]; Acts 1:9; Acts 2:33-36); [I Pet 3:22; Rom 8:34].
h	31.	Rom 8:34;])Heb 9:24([; Heb 7:25.
i	32.	)Rom 14:]9[,10; Acts 1:11(; Acts 10:42; Matt 13:40-42;)Jude 6; II Pet 2:4(; (Matt 16:27; Matt 25:31-33; II Tim 4:1); [John 5:28,29].
k	33.	Rom 5:19;]Heb 9:14,)16([; Heb 10:14; Eph 5:2; Rom 3:25,26.
l	34.	)]Dan 9:24,26[; Col 1:]19[,20(; Eph 1:11,14; John 17:2; Heb 9:12,15; (Rom 5:10,11); [II Cor 5:18,20].
m	35.	)Gal 4:4,5(; Gen 3:15;]Rev 13:8[; Heb 13:8; (see citations under Chapter 7, section 5, figures 9 and 10).
n	36.	Heb 9:14; I Pet 3:18; [(John 10:17,18)].
o	37.	Acts 20:28;]John 3:13; I John 3:16[.
p	38.	John 6:37,39; John 10:]15(,16,[27,28].
q	39.	I John 2:1,])2([; Rom 8:34.
r	40.	John 15:])13([,15; Eph 1:]7,8[,9; John 17:6; (Gal 1:11, 12).
s	41.	)]John 14:16; Heb 12:2[; II Cor 4:13(; Rom 8:9,14; Rom 15:18,19; John 17:17; (Tit 3:4,5).
t	42.	Psa 110:1; I Cor 15:25,26;]Mal 4:2,3[; Col 2:15; [Luke 10:19].

Chapter 9 (PC-11)

a	1.	)Matt 17:12(; James 1:14; Deut 30:19; *John 5:40;* (John 7:17; Rev 22:17); [Acts 7:51; James 4:7];
b	2.	)Eccles 7:29(; Gen 1:26; (see under figure 1 above); [Col 3:10].
c	3.	Gen 2:16,17; Gen 3:6.
d	4.	Rom 5:6; Rom 8:7; John 15:5.
e	5.	Rom 3:[9],10,12,[23]; (Rom 8:7).
f	6.	Eph 2:1,5; Col 2:13.
g	7.	John 6:44,65; I Cor 2:14; Eph 2:2-5; Tit 3:3-5; (Rom 8:8).
h,i	8.	Col 1:13; John 8:34,36; Phil 2:13; Rom 6:18,22.
k	9.	Gal 5:17; Rom 7:15,)]18,19[,21, [22],23(; [I John 1:8,10].

l	10.	)Eph 4:13;]Heb 12;23[(; I John 3:2;)Jude 24(; (Rev 22: 3,4).
	11.	(II Chron 6:36; I John 1:8-10; I John 2:1-6; Psa 17:15).

Chapter 10 (PC-12)

a,b,c	1.	Rom 8:[28],30; Rom 11:7;)Eph 1:[5],10,]11[(; II Thess 2:13,14;)II Cor 3:3,6(; Rom 8:2; II Tim 1:9-10; [John 15:16; Acts 13:48; I Thess 5:9; James 1:18; I Cor 2:12];)Eph 2:1-5(, [6-10].
d	2.	Acts 26:18; I Cor 2:10,12;)Eph 1:17,18(; [II Cor 4:6].
e	3.	Ezek 36:26.
f	4.	Ezek 11:19;]Phil 2:13[; Deut 30:6; Ezek 36:27; (Phil 4: 13); [John 3:5; Gal 6:15; Tit 3:5; I Pet 1:23].
g	5.	])Eph 1:19([; John 6:44,45.
h	6.	)]Cant 1:4[; Psa 110:3(; John 6:37;])Rom 6:16-18([; [Matt 11:28; Rev 22:17]; (see under figure 5 above).
i	7.	II Tim 1:9; Tit 3:4,5;]Eph 2:4,5,8,9[; Rom 9:11.
k	8.	I Cor 2:14; Rom 8:7,[8,9]; Eph 2:5.
l	9.	John 6:37; Ezek 36:27; John 5:25.
m	9a.	)Luke 18:15,16; Acts 2:]38[,39; John 3:]3,5[,[6];]I John 5:12; Rom 8:9[(; [Gen 17:7; Psa 105:8-10; Ezek 16:20, 21; Gal 3:29; Acts 16:15,31-33; I Cor 1:16].
n	9b.	)John 3:8(.
o	10.	)I John 5:12(; Acts 4:12; (John 3:8); [John 16:7,8].
p,q,r	11.	Matt 22:14;)Matt 7:22(; Matt 13,[14,15],20,21; Heb 6: 4,5,(6); John 6:64-66; John 8:24; (I John 2:19); [Acts 28:24].
s	12.	Acts 4:12; John 14:6;)Eph 2:12,[13];]John 4:22[(; John 17:3.
t	13.	II John]9[,10,11;)I Cor 16:22(; Gal 1:])6,7([,8.

Chapter 11 (PC -13)

PCUS renumbered the notes to Chapter 11 to procede consecutively from the last number of Chapter 10 in their 1910 revision.

a	14.	Rom 8:30; Rom 3:24.
b	15.	Rom 4:5-8; II Cor 5:19,21; Rom 3:22,24,25,27,28; Tit 3: 5,7; Eph 1:7; Jer 23:6; I Cor 1:30,31; Rom 5:17-19.

c	16.	)Acts 10:[43],44;]Gal 2:16[(; Phil 3:9; Acts 13:38,39; Eph 2:])7([,8; [John 1:12; John 6:44,45; Phil 1:29].
d	17.	]John 1:12[; Rom 3:28; Rom 5:1; [John 3:16,18,36].
e	18.	James 2:17,22,26; Gal 5:6.
f	19.	Rom 5:8,9,]10[,[18],]19[;)I Tim 2:5,6(; Heb 10:10, 14;])Dan 9:24,26([; Isa 53:])4-6, 10-12([; (I Cor 15:3; II Cor 5:21; I Pet 2:24; I Pet 3:18).
g	20.	Rom 8:32; (John 3:16).
h	21.	II Cor 5:21;)Matt 3:17; Eph 5:2(; (Isa 53:6).
i	22.	Rom 3:24; Eph 1:7; (Rom 6:23; Eph 2:6-9).
k	23.	Rom 3:26; Eph 2:7.
l	24.	)Gal 3:8(; I Pet 1:2,19,20; Rom 8:30.
m	25.	Gal 4:4; I Tim 2:6; Rom 4:25; [I Pet 1:21].
n	26.	)Col 1:21,22(;]Gal 2:16[; Tit 3:4-7; (John 3:5,18,36).
o	27.	Matt 6:12; I John 1:)7(,9; I John 2:1,)2(.
p	28.	Luke 22:32; John 10:28; Heb 10:14; (Phil 1:6; I John 2: 19); [see proofs under Chapter 17].
q	29.	Psa 89:31-33; Psa 51:]7-12[; Psa 32:5; Matt 26:75; I Cor 11:30,32;)Luke 1:20(.
r	30.	Gal 3:(6-8),9,)13(,14;)Rom 4:22-24;]Heb 13:8[(; (Heb 11:13; John 8:56; Acts 15:11; Rom 3:30).

Chapter 12 (PC-14)

a	1.	Eph 1:5; Gal 4:4,5.
b	2.	Rom 8:17; John 1:12.
c	3.	)Jer 14:9; II Cor 6:18(; Rev 3:12.
d	4.	Rom 8:15.
e	5.	Eph 3:12;]Rom 5:2[; [(Heb 4:16)].
f	6.	Gal 4:6.
g	7.	Psa 103:13.
h	8.	Prov 14:26; (Psa 27:1-3).
i	9.	Matt 6:30,32; I Peter 5:7.
k	10.	Heb 12:6.
l	11.	Lam 3:31,[32]; (Heb 13:5).
m	12.	Eph 4:30.
n	13.	Heb 6:12.
o	14.	I Pet 1:)3(,4; Heb 1:14.

Chapter 13 (PC-15)

a,b	1.	])I Cor 6:11([; Acts 20:32;)Phil 3:10(; Rom 6:5,6; John 17:17,[19]; Eph 5:26; II Thess 2:13; [I Cor 1:30].

c	2.	Rom 6:6,14.
d	3.	Gal 5:24; Rom 8:13; (Col 3:5).
e	4.	Col 1:[10],11; Eph 3:16-19; (II Peter 3:13,14).
f	5.	II Cor 7:1; Heb 12:14; [Col 1:28; Col 4:12].
g	6.	I Thess 5:23.
h,i	7.	I John 1:10;]Rom 7:18,23[; Phil 3:12; Gal 5:17;)I Pet 2:11(.
k	8.	Rom 7:23.
i	9.	Rom 6:14; I John 5:4; Eph 4:)15(, 16.
m	10.	II Pet 3:18; II Cor 3:18.
n	11.	II Cor 7:1.

Chapter 14 (PC-16)

a,b	1.	)Heb 10:39; II Cor 4:13; Eph 1:17-19,[20](; Eph 2:8; (I Cor 12:3; Heb 12:2); [see proofs under Chapter 11].
c	2.	Rom 10:14,17; [Matt 28:19,20; I Cor 1:21].
d	3.	I Pet 2:2; Acts 20:32;)Rom 4:11, Luke 17:5; Rom 1:16,17(; (Matt 28:19; I Cor 11:23-29; II Cor 12:8-10); [Luke 22:19; John 6:54-56; Luke 22:32].
e	4.	)John 4:42(; I Thess 2:13; I John 5:10; Acts 24:14.
f	4a.	)Rom 16:26(; [Matt 22:37-40].
g	4b.	)Isa 66:2(.
h	4c.	)Heb 11:13; I Tim 4:8(.
i	4d.	)John 1:12; Acts 16:31; Gal 2:20; Acts 15:11(.
k	5.	])Heb 5:13,14([; Rom 4:19,20; Matt 6:30; Matt 8:10.
l	6.	]Luke 22:31,32[;)Eph 6:16; I John 5:4,5(; (I Cor 10:13).
m	7.	Heb 6:11,12; Heb 10:22;])Col 2:2([; (II Tim 1:12); [see proofs under Chapter 18].
n	8.	Heb 12:2.

Chapter 15 (PC-17)

a	1.	)Zech 12:10(; Acts 11:18.
b	2.	Luke 24:47; Mark 1:15; Acts 20:21.
c	3.	Ezek 18:30,31; Ezek 36:31;])Isa 30:22([; Psa 51:4; Jer 31:18,19;)Joel 2:12,13; Amos 5:15; Psa 119:128(; II Cor 7:11.
d	4.	Psa 119:)6(, 59, 106;)Luke 1:6;]II Kings 23:25[(; (John 14:23); [Matt 21:28,29].
e	5.	)Ezek 36:31,32; Ezek 16:]61,62[,63(; (Tit 3:5; Acts 5:31).
f	6.	)Hos 14:2,4(; Rom 3:24; Eph 1:7.

g	7.	Luke 13:3,)5(; Acts 17:30,)31(.
h	8.	Rom 6:23;])Rom 5:12([; Matt 12:36; (James 2:10).
i	9.	Isa 55:7; Rom 8:1; Isa 1:])16([, 18.
k	10.	Psa 19:13; Luke 19:8; I Tim 1:13,15; (Dan 9; Neh 9).
l	11.	Psa 51:]4,5,7,9,14[; Psa 32:5,6.
m	12.	Prov 28:13; I John 1:9.
n	13.	James 5:16; Luke 17:3,4; Josh 7:19; Psa 51.
o	14.	II Cor 2:(7),8; *Gal 6:1,2*.

Chapter 16 (PC-18)

a	1.	)Micah 6:8; Rom 12:2; Heb 13:21(; (Deut 12:32; Psa 119:9; Matt 28:20; Luke 10:25,26; II Pet 1:19).
b	2.	Matt 15:9; Isa 29:13;)I Pet 1:18; Rom 10:2(; John 16:2; I Sam 15:])21([,22,]23[; [(Col 2:)16,17(,20-23)]; [Deut 10:12,13].
c	3.	James 2:18,22.
d	4.	Psa 116:12,13;)I Pet 2:9(; (Col 3:17; I Chron 29:6-9).
e	5.	I John 2:3,5; II Pet 1:5-10.
f	6.	II Cor 9:2; Matt 5:16; [I Tim 4:12].
g	7.	Tit 2:5,9-12; I Tim 6:1.
h	8.	I Pet 2:15.
i	9.	I Pet 2:12; Phil 1:11; John 15:8.
k	10.	Eph 2:10.
l	11.	Rom 6:22.
m	12.	John 15:)4(,5,6; Ezek 36:26,27; [Luke 11:13].
n	13.	Phil 2:13; Phil 4:13; II Cor 3:5; [Eph 3:16].
o	14.	Phil 2:12; Heb 6:11,12; II Pet 1:3,5,10,11; Isa 64:7; II Tim 1:6;)Acts 26:6,7(; Jude 20, 21.
p	15.	Luke 17:10;])Neh 13:22; Job 9:2,3([; Gal 5:17.
q	16.	Rom 3:20; Rom 4:2,4,6; Eph 2:8,9; Tit 3:5-7; Rom 8:18, [22-24];])Psa 16:2; Job 22:2,3; Job 35:7,8([.
r	17.	)Luke 17:10(; (see citations under 15 above).
s	18.	Gal 5:22,23.
t	19.	Isa 64:6; Gal 5:17; Rom 7:15,18; Psa 143:2; Psa 130:3.
u	20.	Eph 1:6; I Pet 2:5;])Exod 28:38(; Gen 4:4; Heb 11:4[.
w	21.	])Job 9:20([; Psa 143:2; (I Cor 4:3,4).
x	22.	)Heb 13:20,21(; II Cor 8:12; Heb 6:10;)Matt 25:21,23(.
y	23.	II Kings 10:30,31;)I Kings 21:]27[,29(; Phil 1:15,16,18.
z	24.	Gen 4:3-5; Heb 11:4,6.
a	25.	I Cor 13:3; Isa 1:12; [Mark 10:20,21].

b	26.	Matt 6:2,5,16; (Rom 14:23).
c	27.	)Hag 2:14(;]Tit 1:15[;)Amos 5:21,22; Hos 1:4;]Rom 9:16; Tit 3:5[(; (Prov 15:8; Prov 28:9); [Mark 7:6,7].
	28.	)Psa 14:4; Psa 36:3; Job 21:14,15(; Matt 25:41-45; Matt 23:23; (Matt 25:24-28).

Chapter 17 (PC-19)

a	1.	Phil 1:6;]) II Pet 1:10([; John 10:28,29; I John 3:9; I Pet 1:5,9;])*Job 17:9*(; Jer 32:40[.
b	2.	II Tim 2:])18([,19; Jer 31:3; (Eph 1:4,5; John 13:1; Rom 8:35-39).
c	3.	]Heb 10:10,14;)Heb 13:20,21(; Heb 9:12-15[; Rom 8: (32),33,34,]35-37[,38,39; John 17:11,24; Luke 22:32; Heb 7:25.
d	4.	John 14:16,17; I John 2:27; I John 3:9.
e	5.	Jer 32:40; *Heb 8:10-12*.
f	6.	John 10:28; II Thess 3:3; I John 2:19; *I Thess 5:23,24*; (Heb 6:17-20).
g,h	7.	Matt 26:70,72,74;)Psa 51:]Title and[verse 14(; *II Sam 12:9,13*.
i	8.	Isa 64:])5([,7,9; II Sam 11:27.
k	9.	Eph 4:30.
l	10.	Psa 51:8,10,12; Rev 2:4;])Cant 5:2,3,4,6([.
m	11.	)Isa 36:17(; Mark 6:52;])Mark 16:14(; *Psa 95:8*[.
n	12.	Psa 32:3,4; Psa 51:8.
o	13.	II Sam 12:14; (Ezek 16:54).
p	14.	Psa 89:31,32; I Cor 11:32; (II Sam 12:10).

Chapter 18 (PC-20)

a	1.	)]]Job 8:13,14[; Micah 3:11(; Deut 29:19; John 8:41.
b	2.	Matt 7:22,23;])*Job 8:13*([.
c	3.	I John 2:3; I John 3:14,18,19,21,24; I John 5:13; (II Tim 1:12).
d	4.	Rom 5:2,5; (see citations under 3 above); [II Tim 4:7,8].
e	5.	Heb 6:11,(12),)19(; (see citations under 3 and 4 above).
f	6.	Heb 6:17,18; (II Pet 1:4,5).
g	7.	II Pet 1:)4,5(,10,11;)I John 2:3(; I John 3:14;)II Cor 1: 12(.

h	8.	Rom 8:15,16.
i	9.	Eph 1:13,14;)Eph 4:30(; II Cor 1:21,22.
k	10.	I John 5:13;]Isa 50:10;)Mark 9:24([; Psa 88; Psa 77:1-12,(13-20); (Psa 73).
l	11.	I Cor 2:12; I John 4:13;)Heb 6:11,12; Eph 3:17-19(; (Psa 77:10-20; Psa 73; see citations under section 2 above).
m	11a.	II Pet 1:10.
n	11b.	)Rom 5:1,2,5; Rom 14:17; Rom 15:13; Eph 1:3,4; Psa 4:6,7; Psa 119:32(.
o	12.	])I John 2:1,2([; Rom 6:1,2; Tit 2:11,12,14;)II Cor 7:1; Rom 8:1,12; I John 3:2,3;]Psa 130:4[; I John 1:6,7(; (II Pet 1:10).
p	13.	])Cant 5:2,3,6([; Psa 51:8,12,14; Eph 4:30,)]31[(; Psa 77:1-10;]Matt 26:69-72[; Psa 31:22;]Psa 88; Isa 50:10[.
q	14.	I John 3:9; Luke 22:32;])Job 13:15([; Psa 73:15;]Psa 51:8,12; Isa 50:10[.
r	15.	Micah 7:7-9;)Jer 52:40; Isa 54:7-10;]Psa 22:1; Psa 88[(; [II Cor 4:8-10].

Chapter 19 (PC-21)

a	1a.	)Gen 1:26,]27[; Gen 2:17; Rom 2:14,15; Rom 10:5; Rom 5:12,19; Gal 3:10,12;]Eccles 7:29; Job 28:28[(; [Eph 4:24].
b	1.	James 1:25; James 2:8,10,)]11,12[(; Rom 13:8,9; Deut 5:32; Deut 10:4; Exod 34:1; *Rom 3:19;* (Gal 3:12; Hos 6:7; Gen 2:16,17; Compare Rom 5:12-14; I Cor 15:22; Luke 10:25-28; and the covenants made with Noah and Abraham. Gen 1:26; Deut 30:19; John 7:17; Rev 22:17; James 1:14).
c	2.	Matt 22:37-40; *Exod 20:3-18.*
d	3.	Heb 9; Heb 10:1; Gal 4:1-3; Col 2:17.
e	4.	)I Cor 5:7; II Cor 6:17;]Jude 23[(; (see Lev 5:1-6; 6:1-7, and similar passages); [Exod 12:14].
f	5.	Col 2:)14,16(,17;)]]Dan 9:27[[(; Eph 2:15,16; (Mark 7:18, 19; Gal 2:4).
g	6.	Exod 21; Exod 22:)1-29(;)Gen 49:10;]I Pet 2:13,14[; Matt 5:]17[(,(,38,39; I Cor 9:8-10.
h,i	7.	]Rom 13:8,9,)10(;)Eph 6:2([; I John 2:3,4,7,)]8[(;

		Rom 3:31; Rom 6:15;)James 2:[8],10,11(; (see citations under section 2 above); [Rom 3:19].
k	8.	Matt 5:])17([, 18,19;]]James 2:8[; Rom 3:31.
l	9.	Rom 6:14;)]Gal 2:16[; Gal 3:13(; Gal 4:4,5; Acts 13:39; Rom 8:1.
m	10.	Rom 7:12,)22,25(; Psa 119:])4([,5,])6([; I Cor 7:19; Gal 5:14,])16([,18,)19-22(,23.
n	11.	Rom 7:7; Rom 3:20.
o	12.	)James 1:23,]24[,25(; Rom 7:9,14,24.
p	13.	Gal 3:24; Rom 7:24,25; Rom 8:3,4.
q	14.	James 2:11; Psa 119:])101,104([,128.
r	15.	Ezra 9:13,14; Psa 89:30-34.
s	16.	Lev 26:)1(,[2],(3-9),10,(11-13),)14; II Cor 6:16(; Eph 6:2,])3([; Psa 37:11; Matt 5:5; Psa 19:11.
t	16a.	)Gal 2:16; Luke 17:10(.
u	17.	Rom 6:12,14; I Pet 3:8-12; Psa 34:12-16; Heb 12:28,29.
w	18.	)Gal 3:21; *Tit 2:11-14*(; (see citations under section 6 above).
x	19.	)Ezek 36:27; Heb 8:10; Jer 31:33(; (see citations under Chapter 10, section 1; Gal 3:13).

Chapter 20 (PC-22)

a	1.	Tit 2:14; I Thess 1:10;)Gal 3:13(; [Rom 8:1].
b	2.	Gal 1:4;]Col 1:13[; Acts 26:18; Rom 6:14; [I John 1:7].
c	3.	)Rom 8:28(; Psa 119:71; I Cor 15:)54,55(,56,57; Rom 8:1.
d	4.	Rom 5:)1(,2; [Eph 2:18; Eph 3:12; Heb 10:19].
e	5.	Rom 8:14,15; I John 4:18; (Eph 2:18; [Gal 4:6]; Heb 10:19).
f	6.	Gal 3:9,14; (see citations under Chapter 8, section 6).
g	7.	]Gal 4:1-3,6,)7([; Gal 5:1; Acts 15:10,])11([.
h	8.	Heb 4:14,16; Heb 10:19,20,)21,22(.
i	9.	John 7:38,39; II Cor 3:13,17,18; [Rom 5:5].
k,l	10.	)James 4:12(; Rom 14;4,[10]; Acts 4:19; Acts 5:29; I Cor 7:23; Matt 23:8-10; II Cor 1:24; Matt 15:9.
m	11.	Col 2:20,])21([,22,23;)Gal 1:10(; Gal 5:1; Gal 2:(3),4,)5(;])Psa 5:1([; [Gal 4:9,10].
n	12.	))]Rom 10:17[; Rom 14:23; Isa 8:20; Acts 17:11; John 4:22(;]Hos 5:11; Rev 13:12,16,17[;)Jer 8:9(; [I Pet 3:15].

o   13.   Gal 5:13; I Pet 2:16; II Pet 2:19; John 8:34; Luke 1:74,75; [Rom 6:15; II Pet 3:15].

p   14.   ])Matt 12:25([; I Pet 2:13,14,16; Rom 13:1-8; Heb 13:17.

q   15.   ])Rom 1:32([; I Cor 5:]1,5[,11,[12],13;])II John 5:10, 11([; II Thess 3:14;])I Tim 6:3-5(; Tit 1:)10,11(,13[; Tit 3:10; Matt 18:)15,16(,17,(18);])ITim 1:19,20; Rev 2:14,15,20; Rev 3:9([; [Rom 16:17; II Thess 3:6].

        15a.   ])Deut 13:6-12; Rom 13:3,4; II John 5:10,11; Ezra 7: 23-28; Rev 17:12,16,17; Neh 13:15,17,21,22,25,30; II Kings 23:5,6,9,20,21; II Chron 34:33; II Chron 15: 12,13,16; Dan 3:29; I Tim 2:2; Isa 49:23; Zech 13:2,3([*—omitted by AmEd along with the passage in the text it supports; see the last entry under 20.4 in Appendix I.*

Chapter 21 (PC-23)

a   1.   Rom 1:(19),20;)]Acts 17:24[; Psa 119:68(; Jer 10:7;)Psa 31:23; Psa 18:3; Rom 10:12; Psa 62:8; Josh 24:14; Mark 12:33(; (Psa 19:1-6); [Acts 14:17].

b   2.   Deut 12:32; Matt 15:9;]Acts 17:(24),25[; Matt 4:9,10;]Deut 4:15-20[; Exod 20:4-6;]Col 2:(20-)23[; [John 4: 23,24].

c   3.   Matt 4:10; John 5:23; II Cor 13:14; *Rev. 5:11-13,*[14]; [Matt 28:19].

d   4.   Col 2:18; Rev 19:10; Rom 1:25.

e   5.   John 14:6; I Tim 2:5; Eph 2:18;)Col 3:17(.

f   6.   Phil 4:6; [I Tim 2:1; Col 4:2].

g   7.   )Psa 65:2(; (Luke 18:1; I Tim 2:8); [Psa 67:3; I Thess 5: 17,18].

h   8.   John 14:13,14;)I Pet 2:5(.

i   9.   Rom 8:26; [Eph 6:18].

k   10.   I John 5:14.

l   11.   Psa 47:7;])Eccles 5:1,2([; Heb 12:28; Gen 18:27; James 5:16; James 1:6,7; Mark 11:24; Matt 6:12,14,15;]Col 4:2[; Eph 6:18.

m   12.   I Cor 14:14.

n   13.   ]I John 5:14[; [Matt 26:42].

o   14.   I Tim 2:1,2; John 17:20; II Sam 7:29;)]Ruth 4:12[(.

p   15.   )II Sam 12:21-23; Luke 16:25,26;]Rev 14:13[(; (this statement is based on the absence of any command to pray for the dead, and of any example in the Scripture of such prayer; I John 5:14).

q	16.	)I John 5:16(.
r	17.	Acts 15:21; Rev 1:3; (Acts 17:11).
s	18.	II Tim 4:2.
t	19.	James 1:22; Acts 10:33; Matt 13:19; Heb 4:2; Isa 66:2.
u	20.	Col 3:16; Eph 5:19; James 5:13; [Acts 16:25].
w	21.	Matt 28:19; I Cor 11:23-29; Acts 2:42.
x	22.	Deut 6:13;)Neh 10:29(.
y	23.	]Isa 19:21[; [Eccles 5:4,5];])Acts 18:18([; (Psa 116:14; Neh 10:29).
z	24.	Joel 2:12;]Esther 4:16[; Matt 9:15;]I Cor 7:5[; [Mat 6:17,18].
a	25.	Psa 107;])Esther 9:22([; [Neh 12:31-43].
b	26.	)Heb 12:28(; (John 4:24; Heb 10:22).
c	27.	John 4:21.
d	28.	Mal 1:11; I Tim 2:8.
e	29.	John 4:23,24.
f	30.	)Jer 10:25(; Deut 6:)6(,7; Job 1:5;)II Sam 6:18,20;]I Pet 3:7(; Acts 10:2[.
g	31.	Matt 6:11;)]*Josh 24:15*[(; [Dan 6:10].
h	32.	Matt 6:6;]Eph 6:18[; [Neh 1:4-11].
i	33.	Isa 56:7; Heb 10:25;)]Prov 1:20,21,24[; Prov 8:34(;]Acts 13:42; Luke 4:16[; Acts 2:42.
k	34.	Exod 20:8,[(9)],10,11; Isa 56:2,4,6,)]7[(.
l,m,n	35.	)Gen 2:]2[,3(; I Cor 16:1,2; Acts 20:7;)Rev 1:10; Exod 20:8,10; Matt 5:17,18(; (these texts are cited in connection with the example of the apostles and the early church.)
o	36.	)]Exod 20:8[(; Exod 16:23,25,26,29,30; Exod 31:15,16,)]17[(; Isa 58:13; Neh 13:15-22; (Luke 23:56).
p	37.	Isa 58:13; Matt 12:1-13.

Chapter 22 (PC-24)

a	1.	Deut 10:20.
b	2.	Exod 20:7;)Lev 19:12(; II Cor 1:23; II Chron 6:22,23.
c	3.	Deut 6:13.
d	4.	Exod 20:7; Jer 5:7; Matt 5:)34(,37; James 5:12.
ef	5.	)Heb 6:16; II Cor 1:23; Isa 65:16(; I Kings 8:31;])Neh 13:25([; Ezra 10:5; (Matt 26:63,64).

g,h	6.	)Exod 20:7; Jer 4:2; Gen 24:2,3,]5,6,8[,9;]Numb 5:19, 21; Neh 5:12; Exod 22:7-11[(; (see citations under Section 2 above).
k	7.	Jer 4:2; Psa 24:4; [Ex 20:7].
l	8.	)]I Sam 25:22,32-34[(; Psa 15:4.
m	9.	Ezek 17:16,18,)]19[(; Josh 9:18,19; II Sam 21:1.
n	10.	)Isa 19:21; Eccles 5:4-6(; Psa 61:8; Psa 66:13,14; (Deut 23:21,23).
o	11.	Psa 76:11; Jer 44:25,26.
p	12.	)Deut 23:21,23(; Psa 50:14;]Gen 28:20-22[; I Sam 1:11;)]Psa 66:13,14[(; Psa 132:2-5.
q	13.	)Acts 23:12,]14[; Mark 6:26(;]Numb 30:5,8,12,13[.
r	13a.	)]Matt 19:11,12[; I Cor 7:2,9; Eph 4:28;]I Pet 4:2[; I Cor 7:23(; [I Thess 4:11,12].

Chapter 23 (PC-25)

a	1.	Rom 13:1,)2(,3,4; I Pet 2:13, 14.
b	2.	Prov 8:15,16;)Rom 13:1,2,[3],4(; (see citations under Section 1 above).
c	3.	])Psa 2:10-12; I Tim 2:2([; Psa 82:3,4;)II Sam 23:3(; I Pet 2:13; [Psa 101]; (see citations under Section 1 above).
d	4.	Luke 3:14; Rom 13:(1-)4; Matt 8:9,)10(;]Acts 10:1,2;)Rev 17:14,16([.
e,f,g	5.	II Chron 26:18;])Matt 18:17([; Matt 16:19;])I Cor 12: 28,29([; Eph 4:11,12; I Cor 4:1,)2(;)]Rom 10:15[; Heb 5:4(; [(John 18:36); Acts 5:29].
h,i	5a.	)Isa 49:23;]Psa 122:9; Ezra 7:23-28; Lev 24:16; Deut 13: 5,6,12; II Kings 18:4; I Chron 13:1-9; II Kings 23:1-26; II Chron 34:33; II Chron 15:12,13 [(. [Rom 13:1-6; Psa 105:15; Acts 18:14-16].
k	6.	])II Chron 19:8-11; II Chron 29 and 30; Matt 2:4,5([; [II Sam 23:3; Rom 13:4]; (see General Note).
l	7.	I Tim 2:1,2,[3].
m	8.	I Pet 2:17.
n	9.	Rom 13:6,7; [Matt 22:21].
o	10.	Rom 13:5; Tit 3:1.
p	11.	)I Pet 2:13,14,16(; (this is an inference from the duties just stated).
q	12.	Rom 13:1;])I Kings 2:35([; Acts 25:])9([,10,11;])II Pet

2:1,10,11; Jude 8-11([.

r   13.   ])II Thess 2:4; Rev 13:15-17([; [II Tim 2:24; I Pet 5:3];
(this is an inference from the doctrine of the civil
magistrate, and from duties incumbent on believers
with respect to him).

Chapter 24 (original)

*The original 1647 Chapter 24 and its 1797 American counterpart had
15 notes. After 1861 PCUS combined notes 6 and 7 at the end of
paragraph 3 as note 6. Original note 10 (Lev 20:19-21) disappeared in
both PCUS and PCUSA versions along with the passage it supported at
the end of paragraph 4 (see Appendix I), but PCUS added the citation to
the previous note.*

a   1.   Gen 2:24;)Matt 19:[4],5,6;]Prov 2:17(; *I Cor 7:2;*
                  Mark 10:6-9[; [(Rom 7:3)].

b   2.   Gen 2:18.

c   3.   Mal 2:15; [(Gen 9:1)].

d   4.   I Cor 7:2,9.

e   5.   Heb 13:4; I Tim 4:3;)]I Cor 7:36-38[; Gen 24:57-58(.

f,g   6.   I Cor 7:39;]Gen 34:14; Exod 34:16[;)Deut 7:3,4(;
                  I Kings 11:4; Neh 13:25-27;])Mal˙2:11,12([; II Cor 6:14.

h   7.   Lev 18; I Cor 5:1;])Amos 2:7([.

i   8.   Mark 6:18; Lev 18:24-28; Lev 20:19-21.

k   9.   )Matt 1:18-20(; (Deut 22:23).

l   10.   Matt 5:31,32.

m   11.   Matt 19:9;)Rom 7:2,3(.

n   12.   Matt 19:8,])9([; I Cor 7:15; Matt 19:6.

o   13.   Deut 24:1-4; *Ezra 10:3.*

Chapter 24 (current PC-26)

1.   Gen 2:23,24; I Cor 7:2,39; Matt 19:4-6; Eph 5:28,31,33;
      I Cor 13:8,13; Matt 5:31,32; Mark 10:5-9; Rom 7:2,3.

2.   Gen 2:18,24.

3.   Gen 1:27,28; Eph 5:22,23; Col 3:18,19; Gen 2:18-25;
      I Cor 7:3-5,9,36.

4.   Gen 1:27,28; Gen 9:1; Mal 2:15; Matt 18:5,6,10,14;
      Matt 19:14; Eph 6:1-4; Col 3:20,21; Mark 10:13-16;

Luke 18:15-17.

5. Gen 1:27,28.

6. Mark 6:18; I Cor 5:1; Lev 18:6-18.

7. Mark 1:30; John 2:1,2; I Tim 5:14; Heb 13:4; I Cor 7:7, 36; I Cor 9:5; I Tim 4:3.

8. I Cor 7, especially v. 39; II Cor 6:14,15.

9. Prov 18:22; Matt 19:6; Eph 5:29,30,32; Mark 10:9,11,12.

10. Gen 1:27,28.

11. Mark 10:9.

12. Eph 5:22,23.

13. Gen 2:23-24; Matt 5:31,32; Mark 10:5-9; Rom 7:2,3; I Cor 7:2,10,11,39; Eph 5:28,31,33; Matt 19:4-9; I Cor 13:4-13.

14. Mark 10:4-9; I Cor 7:12,13,15; Matt 19:7-9.

15. II Sam 12:13; Neh 9:17; Psa 32:5; Psa 130:4; Matt 12: 31a; Matt 21:31,32; John 8:3,11; Rom 3:23; Gal 6:1; I Tim 2:4; Heb 7:25; I John 1:9; I John 2:1,2; Luke 7:36-50; Luke 15:11-32; John 3:16,17; Rom 10:9,10.

16. Matt 5:31,32; I Cor 7:10,11,20,32-35; Mark 10:11; Luke 16:18.

Chapter 25 (PC-27)

a   1. Eph 1:)10(,22,23; Eph 5:23,27,32; Col 1:18.

b   2. I Cor 1:2; I Cor 12:12,13;)Psa 2:8,]Rev 7:9[(; Rom 15: 9-12.

c   3. I Cor 7:14; Acts 2:39;)]Ezek 16:20,21[; Rom 11:16;]Gen 3:15[(; Gen 17:7; *Gal 3:7,9,14; Rom 4;* (Mark 10: 13-16).

d   4.]Matt 13:47[; Isa 9:7; [(Col 1:13); Matt 13:31; Psa 72].

e   5. Eph 2:19;)Eph 3:15;]*Prov 29:18*[(.

f   6.)Acts 2:47(; (Matt 28:19; Acts 2:38; I Cor 12:13; Matt 26: 26-28); [Matt 10:32,33].

g   7.]I Cor 12:23[(; Eph 4:11-13; Matt 28:19,20; Isa 59:21.

h   8. Rom 11:3,4;)]Rev 12:6,14[(; *Acts 9:31.*

i   9. Rev 2 and 3; I Cor 5:6,7; [Acts 2:41,42].

k   10. [I Cor 5];)I Cor 13:12; Rev 2 and 3(; Matt 13:24-30,47, (48); [I Cor 1:2].

l   11.]Rev 18:2[; Rom 11:]18,19[,20-22; [Rev 2:9].

m   12. Matt 16:18;]Psa 102:28[; Matt 28:19,20;)Psa 72:]17[(.

n   13. Col 1:18;)Eph 1:22(.

o   13a.)Matt 23:8-10; II Thess 2:3,4,]8,9; Rev 13:6[(; [I Pet 5: 2-4].

Chapter 26 (PC-28)

a 1. I John 1:3; Eph 3:16,17,]18,19[; John 1:16;)]Eph 2:5, 6[(; Phil 3:10; Rom 6:5,6;)]II Tim 2:12[(; [(Rom 8:17)].

b 2. Eph 4:15,16;)]I Cor 12:7; I Cor 3:21-23; Col 2:19[(; (I John 1:3,7).

c 3. I Thess 5:11,14;)]Rom 1:11,12,14[(; I John 3:16-18; Gal 6:10.

d 4. Heb 10:24,25; Acts 2:42,46;)Isa 2:3(; I Cor 11:20.

e 5.)]Acts 2:44,45[(; I John 3:17; II Cor 8 and 9; Acts 11:29, 30.

f 6. Col 1:18)]19[(; I Cor 8:6;)]Isa 42:8[; I Tim 6:15,16; Psa 45:7;] Heb 1:8,9[(; (Psa 14:7).

g 7.)]Exod 20:15; Eph 4:28[(; Acts 5:4.

Chapter 27 (PC-29)

a,b 1.)Rom 4:11(; Gen 17:)7(, (9),10,(11);)Matt 28:19; I Cor 11:23(; (Exod 13:9,10; Exod 12:3-20).

c 2. I Cor 10:16; I Cor 11:25,26; Gal 3:27.

d 3.)]Rom 15:8[(; Exod 12:48;)]Gen 34:14[; *I Cor 10:21*(; (Heb 13:10; I Cor 11:27-29).

e 4. Rom 6:3,4; I Cor 10:[2], (14,15),16,)]21[(; (see context).

f 5. Gen 17:10; Matt 26:27,28; Tit 3:5.

g,h 6. Rom 2:28,29;)I Pet 3:21; Matt 3:11; I Cor 12:13(; (I Cor 3:7; I Cor 6:11; John 3:5; Acts 8:13-23).

i 7.)]Matt 26:27,28; Matt 28:19,20[(; (John 6:63); [Luke 22: 19,20; I Cor 11:26].

k 8. Matt 28:19; I Cor 11:20,23;)I Cor 4:1; Heb 5:4(;

   9. (see General Note.)

l 10.)I Cor 10:1-4(;]*I Cor 5:7,8*[; (Col 2:11,12).

Chapter 28 (PC-30)

a 1. Matt 28:19;)]*Mark 16:16*[(.

b 2.)I Cor 12:13; *Gal 3:27,28*(; (Acts 2:41; Acts 10:47).

c 3. Rom 4:11; Col 2:11,12; (Gal 3:29).

d 4. Gal 3:27; Rom 6:(3,4),)5(.

e 5. Tit 3:5.

f 6. Mark 1:4; *Acts 2:38; Acts 22:16*.

g	7.	Rom 6:3,4.
h	8.	Matt 28:19,20.
i	9.	)]Matt 3:11; John 1:33[(; Matt 28:19,)]20[(; *Acts 10:47; Acts 8:36,38;* (Eph 4:11-13).
	10.	(see General Note).
k	11.	]Heb 9:10,19-21,)22([;)Acts 2:41; Acts 16:33(;]Mark 7:4[; (Acts 1:5; Acts 2:3,4,17; Acts 11:15,16); [Acts 10: 46,47; I Cor 10:2].
l	12.	)]Mark 16:15,16; Acts 8:37,38[(; (see citations under Section 1 above); [Acts 9:18].
m	13.	Gen 17:7,9,(10); Gal 3:9,14;]Col 2:11,12[; Acts 2:38,39; Rom 4:11,12; I Cor 7:14;])Matt 28:19(; Mark 10:13-16; Luke 18:15[,(16); *Acts 16:14,15,33.*
n	14.	Luke 7:30;)Exod 4:24-26(; (Gen 17:14); [Deut 28:9].
o	15.	Rom 4:11; Acts 10:)2,4,22,31(,45,(46),47; (Luke 23:40-43).
p	16.	Acts 8:13,23.
q	17.	John 3:5,8; (Rom 4:11).
r	18.	Gal 3:27;)]Tit 3:5[(; Eph 5:25,26; Acts 2:38,(39,40),41; (Eph 1:4,5; Acts 16:31,33).
s	19.	)Tit 3:5(. (There is no command, and no adequate example for the repetition of baptism.)

Chapter 29 (PC-31)

a	1.	I Cor 11:23-26; I Cor 10:16,17,21; I Cor 12:13; (Matt 26: 26,27; Luke 22:19,20).
b	1a.	Heb 9:22,25,26,28.
c	1b.	)I Cor 11:24-26(; Matt 26:26,27: *Luke 22:19-20.*
d	2.	)Heb 7:23,24,27(; Heb 10:11,12,14,18.
e	3.	)Matt 26:26-28; Mark 14:22-24; Luke 22:19,20; I Cor 11: 23-27(; (see citations under Sections 1,2).
f	3a.	)Acts 20:7; I Cor 11:20(.
g	3b.	)]I Cor 10:6[(; [I Tim 1:3-4].
h	3c.	)]Mark 4:23[; I Cor 11:25-29(.
i	4.	Matt 15:9; (there is not the least appearance of a warrant for any of these things, either in precept or example, in any part of the word of God; see all the places in which the ordinance is mentioned).
k	5.	Matt 26:26-28.
l	6.	I Cor 11:26,27,)28(;])Matt 26:29([.
m	7.	)Acts 3:21; I Cor 11:24-26; Luke 24:6,39(; (these state-

ments are inferences from the doctrine of the sacraments and do not require specific Scripture proofs).

n,o   8.)I Cor 11:28;]*I Cor 5:7,8*[(; I Cor 10:16;)*I Cor 10:3,4*(;
            (John 6:53,58; see note under Section 6 above).

p,q   9. I Cor 11:27,)]28[(,29;)II Cor 6:14-16(; *I Cor 10:21*;
            I Cor 5:6,7,13; II Thess 3:6,14,15;)Matt 7:6(.

Chapter 30 (PC-32)

a   1. Isa 9:6,7; I Tim 5:17;)I Thess 5:12; Acts 20:17,28;]Heb
          13:7,17,24[(; I Cor 12:28;)]Matt 28:18-20; *Psa 2:6-9*[(;
          John 18:36.
b   2. Matt 16:19; Matt 18:17,18; John 20:21-23; II Cor 2:6-8.
c   3. I Cor 5; I Tim 5:20;)]Matt 7:6[(; I Tim 1:20; I Cor 11:27-
          34; Jude 23; (II Sam 12:14).
d   4. I Thess 5:12; II Thess 3:6,14,)15(; I Cor 5:4,5,13; Matt
          18:17; Tit 3:10.

Chapter 31 (PC-33)

a   1.   Acts 15:(1),2,(3),4,(5),6,(7-41); [Rev 2:1-6; Acts 20:
           17,28].
b,c   1a.)]Isa 49:23; I Tim 2:1,2; II Chron 19:8-11; II Chron 29,
           30; Matt 2:4,5; Prov 11:14; Acts 15:2,4,22,23,25[(;
           [Acts 15; Acts 20:17].
d   2.   Acts 15:15,19,24,27-31; Acts 16:4; Matt 18:17-19,]20[,
           [29].
e   3.   )Eph 2:20; Acts 17:11; I Cor 2:5; II Cor 1:24(; (see
           General Note).
f   4.   Luke 12:13,14; John 18:36; [(Matt 22:21)].

Chapter 32 (PC-34)

a   1. Gen 3:19; Acts 13:36.
b   2. Luke 23:43;)Eccles 12:7(; (Phil 1:23; II Cor 5:6-8).
c   3.)]Heb 12:23[; II Cor 5:1,]6[,8; Phil 1:23; Acts 3:21; Eph
          4:10;]*I John 3:2*[(; (Luke 16:23; [Rom 8:23]; see under
          Figure 2 above); [Rev 7:4,15].
d   4. Luke 16:23,24;)]Acts 1:25[; Jude 6,7;]I Pet 3:19[(;

		(II Pet 2:9).
e	5.	I Thess 4:17; I Cor 15:51,52.
f	6.	)]Job 19:26,27[(; I Cor 15:42-44; (see preceding context).
g	7.	Acts 24:15; John 5:28,29;)]I Cor 15:42[(; Phil 3:21.

Chapter 33 (PC-35)

a	1.	Acts 17:31; (Matt 25:31-34).
b	2.	John 5:22,27.
c,d	3.	)]I Cor 6:3[(; Jude 6; II Pet 2:4; II Cor 5:10;)Eccles 12:14(; Rom 2:16; Rom 14:10,12; Matt 12:36,37; (I Cor 3:13-15).
e	4.	Rom 9:23;)Matt 25:21(; (Eph 2:4-7).
f	5.	Rom 2:5,6; II Thess 1:7,8,)Rom 9:22(.
g	6.	Matt 25:31-34;)Acts 3:19(; II Thess 1:7; (Psa 16:11).
h	7.	Matt 25:41,46; II Thess 1:9;)]*Isa 66:24*[(; [(Mark 9:]47[,48)].
i	8.	II Pet 3:11,14; II Cor 5:])10([,11; II Thess 1:5-7; Luke 21:27,28;)]Rom 8:23-25[(.
k	9.	Matt 24:36,42-44; Mark 13:35-37; Luke 12:35,36; Rev 22:20.

Chapter 34 (PC-9)

This and the following chapter, the new chapters on the Holy Spirit and the Gospel, are annotated in the PCUS text by paragraph only rather than by specific statements within paragraphs.

a,b,c,d	1.	II Cor 13:14; John 15:26; Matt 28:19; Matt 3:16,17;]Luke 1:35[; Eph 4:30;]Heb 10:29; I Cor 10:10,11; Rev 22:17[; Eph 2:18]-20,22[; John 14:26;]John 16:7[; Gal 4:[4,5],6; Acts 5:3,4; Acts 16:]6[,7;]Mark 3:29; Rom 8:26,27; I John 2:20-27[; [Acts 2:33; John 20:22; Rom 8:14; I Thess 5:19; John 4:24].
e,f,g	2.	]Eph 4:30; Eph 5:9[; Gen 1:2; John 3:5,[7];]Acts 2:1-21[; Gal 5:22,23,]24,25[; John 16:8,9,]10,11[; II Peter 1:21; II Tim 3:16; I Cor 2:[9],10,[13];]I Pet 1: 11[; John 16:13,14],15[;]Acts 7:51[; I Thess 5:19; Psa 104:30; [Psa 139:7; Acts 28:25; Acts 1:8; Acts 2:7; Rom

8:9,14-16; Tit 3:5,6; Rom 5:5; Matt 12:31,32].

h,i,k   3.   ]John 3:1-8[; Acts 2:38; Luke 11:13;]I Cor 12:3; John
7:37-39; John 16:13[; John 16:7,8,]9-11[; Rev 22:17;
Titus 3:5,6]7[; II Thess 2:13;]Gal 4:6; I John 4:2[;
Rom 8:]14[,[15,16],]17[,26,]27[; Eph 4:30;]I Cor 2:13,
14[; [Eph 1:13; I Thess 1:5; Gal 6:8; Eph 2:18; Eph 5:9
Eph 4:3; Jude 20,21; Rom 15:16; Heb 10;14,15;
I Cor 6:19; I Cor 3:16].

l,m,n,o   4.   ]Eph 2:14-18[; Eph 4:]1-3[,4-6,[30]; Eph 5:18; Acts 2:4;
Acts 13:2,[3]; I Cor 12:[4-13];]II Pet 1:19-21; I Thess
1:5,6; John 20:22,23[; Matt 28:19,]20[; [Acts 20:28;
Acts 6:3,5,6; Gal 5:16,22,23; II Tim 3:16; John 16:13,14;
I Cor 2:10; Rev 2:7; Acts 1:8; Rev 22:17].

Chapter 35 (PC-10)

a,b,c,   1.   ]Rev 22:17; John 3:16; I John 2:1,2; Acts 2:38,39[; Matt
d,e,f   11:28,29,]30[;]II Cor 5:14-19[; Tit 2:11;]Heb 2:9; Luke
24:46,47[; [Jer 31:3; I John 4:9,16; Tit 3:4,5; Heb 13:
20,21; Heb 12:22-24; Heb 8:10; Eph 2:8; I Tim 2:5,6;
Heb 9:26; I Cor 15:3; Rom 5:6,8; John 10:10,11; John
11:25; John 14:6,19; Phil 1:21; Acts 4:12; Rom 1:16;
Heb 5:9; II Pet 3:9; Matt 24:14; John 4:42; Rev 11:15;
Rom 6:23; II Cor 9:15].

g,h,i,j,k   2.   ]Matt 28:19,20; Acts 4:12; John 6:37-40[; John 17:3;
Acts 16:[30],31; Acts 2:38;]Gal 2:16-20; Rom 1:16,17;
Rom 4:5; Acts 13:38,39, 48[; II Pet 3:9;]Matt 11:28-30[;
Mark 1:]14[,15; Acts 17:30; Rev 22:17;]Ezek 33:11; Isa
1:18; Luke 13:34[; [John 3:16,17; I John 4:9,10; Isa 45:
22; Heb 10:19-22; John 14:6; Rom 10:9; I Pet 1:8,9; Heb
3:7,8; II Cor 6:2; Heb 4:16; Rom 5:8; II Thess 3:5; Phil
2:12,13; John 16:13,14].

l,m   3.   Heb 2:3,]Heb 12:25; Acts 13:46; Matt 10:32,33; Luke
12:47,48; Heb 10:29[; [I Thess 5:9,10; John 1:12; Heb
4:16; Rev 22:17; I Tim 6:12; John 3:18; Matt 25:46;
Rom 6:23].

n,o,p,q,   4.   Acts 4:12; Matt 28:19,20; Acts 1:8; Rom 10:13-15,
r,s,t,u   [16,17]; Heb 10:]19-22[,23-25;]Gal 3:28; I Cor 16:1,2[;
Matt 9:]36,37[,38;]Acts 13:2-4; Col 3:16; Rev 22:17;
Col 1:28,29[; [Acts 16:31; II Tim 3:15; John 5:39; Matt
24:14; Matt 13:38; John 17:18; Acts 20:28; I Pet 5:2;

John 21:15,16; I Cor 3:9; I Cor 11:24; II Cor 1:11; Eph 6:18,19; Heb 13:16; Gal 6:6; Matt 10:8; II Cor 9:7; II Tim 2:15; Rom 12:11; Col 3:23,24; Matt 6:10,13; Rev 11:15].